Who's Making
MONEY
at Digital/Inkjet Printing
...and how?

Bill Farquharson & Kelly Mallozzi

Table of Contents

Introduction:

What this book is, is not, and how to use it.

What you're holding in your hands right now can best be described as a sales playbook for digital and production inkjet printing. No, wait, it's a collection of sales tips that will point you toward digital/inkjet profitability. Hmmmm ... maybe it's something of a memoir, written by two former digital printing salespeople (one of whom also has experience selling the equipment) who've been passionately giving advice about the power of digital and inkjet output since the day the earth cooled (or the early '90s when digital equipment started landing in print shops everywhere). Or perhaps it's the answer to the oft-heard question, "When are you two going to write a book?" Whatever it is, the target market for this advice, and therefore the book, is simple: Anyone currently selling digital/inkjet printing or who is thinking about jumping into the digital printing pool. Primarily, we're talking to you, sales person or selling owner. But equipment manufacturers, in-plants, and, well, *you* could get something out of this as well.

Now, when we say, "Who's making money at digital/inkjet printing...and how?, we are talking about the kind of money that shows up in a commission check that a sales rep would receive. Since we, the authors, are salespeople at heart, we write with a sales-focus. We both found career success and made a comfortable living in the world of digital print, so we want to help you do the same.

The secondary use of this book is to offer information on a Production/Operations level, and discuss what the best of the best are doing. From years of immersion in the technology and content creation on the subject of digital printing profitability, we have come across some excellent, best-case practices to share.

However, you will not find ratios and financial data supporting the cost of the equipment. While important, that information is boring and, as salespeople, we'd nod off at the keyboard faster than you can say, "Monthly sales meeting." Nope. This book is devoid of pie charts, graphs, or trends and predictions. Someone else can teach you which piece of equipment to buy, digital press speeds and feeds, etc. Our goal is to help you make more money.

How will this be accomplished?

As the saying goes, "Success leaves clues." That is, every challenge you are facing in your business has already been solved by someone else. Knowing that, why suffer? Why not learn from those who've gone before you and benefit from their experiences? Because we have both sold digital printing and worked hard to make companies who have installed digital/inkjet printing equipment successful, we are the Farmers Insurance of digital print: We know a thing or two, because we've seen a thing or two.

We'll start with some realities and truths — things that industry vendors might not tell you, but we will. For example, would it surprise you to learn that, if given a choice between selling digital print and enduring elective root canal, your print salespeople would rather be on the phone making a dentist appointment? Typical sales reps have zero interest in something they consider to be minuscule sales opportunities that yield even more "minuscule-r" commissions.

We'll teach you how to change that attitude, showing you not only how to get their attention, but also how to turn them into digital sales dynamos.

Next, we'll cover the common denominators that are found among the most successful and profitable digital print providers in the industry. But be forewarned: You will be grateful for the information, but don't expect any groundbreaking, forehead-slapping, "Why-didn't-I-think-of-that?" revelations. It's not rocket surgery. Rather, it's a lot of common sense, planning, preparation and simple execution (the key word being "simple"). It ain't complicated, so don't over-think it. The "best of the best" aren't doing anything extraordinary. They are just adhering to the basic rules of sales. They are identifying customer business needs and using their digital/inkjet printing technology capabilities to fulfill them. And here's the cool part: They're not competing for business based on price. In fact, price is only brought up when the client needs a dollar amount to put on the Purchase Order.

We'll show you how to achieve that, helping you to build a brand and reputation centered around problem-solving, resulting in an invitation to sit at the customer's "Cool Table," where the decisions, planning and ideas are formed.

And then, we'll provide you with an action plan so that you are clear on what you need to do in order to go from where you currently are in the digital printing sales process to where you need to be. There is one message for owners/presidents and another for sales people.

At the core of this book is a lot of talk about Sales and Marketing. And vertical markets? Yup. We'll end the book by providing detailed instructions on how to sell digital print profitably and successfully to several industries, covering:

a. Banks and Credit Unions
b. Churches
c. Hospitals/Medical Centers
d. Colleges and Secondary Schools
e. Restaurants
f. Non-Profits

If you are already selling digital/inkjet printing, this book will get you to the next level. If you are on the sidelines studying your options, we'll give you some food for thought and provide answers to the challenges you are certain to face.

Quick side note: While there are plenty of ideas and tips for selling digital printing successfully, this book is not a "how to sell" guide. If there are nuances to selling digital/inkjet printing, we'll mention them. That is, we dive into prospecting and pitching digital printing solutions, but for the more granular fundamentals of selling (and especially selling print), check out Bill Farquharson's wicked-good new, "The 25 Best Print Sales Tips Ever!" book, now available on Amazon.

If you haven't gone digital, why you should.

Dr. Joe Webb once said, "Printers do not adopt any new technology until they start losing business to it." That quote might be a slight on the business acumen of print shop owners, but it's not inaccurate. Ours has been a reactive industry, rather than one that looks forward and takes a chance on unproven technology. Not surprisingly, then, it's the risk takers and forward thinkers who have survived and thrived. And the "It's just a fad" crowd are the ones who now find themselves wondering what happened.

Digital printing — the concept of printing directly from an electronic file — first hit the collective consciousness of the printing industry in the early 1990s. Back then, it was called "on-demand printing" for obvious reasons: Customers could only get what they needed when they needed it. Industry vendors, consultants, trade show promoters and the rags made all kinds of predictions for explosive digital printing growth and immediate profitability for those printers who embraced it, largely with self-serving boldness. Turns out, they were half right and way too early with their predictions.

There was growth, but it was not rapid at first and most of the early adopters learned firsthand what the phrase "bleeding edge" really means. It's funny now, but there were once hours-long seminars on how to make PDF files! We all gasped and applauded when it was predicted that, one day, this would be a quick, two-keystroke process. What's next, we thought, ordering print directly from a website?

A good many printers got into digital printing for the wrong reasons and, subsequently, took a financial bath. They drank the Kool-Aid and believed the hype. They saw the hockey stick-shaped growth predictions and bought into the "If you buy it, they will come" can't-miss sales pitch. While everyone involved promoted and raved about the on-demand opportunity, there weren't enough experts who saw what was happening in the correct light. It was the Emperor's New Clothes all over again: "Digital printing is coming and, if you don't see it, you're a fool. Get into digital now!" No wonder there was such a high failure rate early on.

Funny and completely true story:

In 1998, I (Bill) was in Melbourne, Australia, at a print conference along with a few other American experts and early adopters of digital printing technology. Bob Hall, then-editor of Quick Printing magazine, was at the microphone handling introductions. He introduced me like this: *"Bill Farquharson is here from Boston (applause). Bill once told me that digital printing is like having sex in high school. Everyone thinks everyone else is doing it but not many people are really doing it. And those who are, aren't doing it very well."* Yeah, that sounds like something I would say! To make things even more embarrassing, I had brought my 74-year-old mother with me on the trip. I think she sent me to my hotel room early that night.

Today, not only has the commercial printing industry fully embraced the opportunities that come from digital/inkjet printing, but other graphic arts segments have also joined the chorus, most notably labels, wide-format, packaging and screen printing. Still, some printing companies remain unmoved. Perhaps their clients aren't asking for it, so they aren't going to pull the trigger on what they consider to be a newfangled device.

If this is you, perhaps you should look to your personal life for proof that embracing digital printing is necessary. Consider your banking habits. Gone are the days when checks were deposited in-person and bills were paid through the mail. Now, bills are paid electronically. Your vendors' billing information has been captured by the bank (right down to the account numbers), thanks to the considerable time investment you put into setting it all up. Having gone through all that work, what would it take to change banks? How excited are you to do it all over again? It will likely take more than a free toaster and a couple of cat calendar giveaways to make a switch. The translation to our industry is this: Own the digital file and you will own the customer. But more on this topic later.

If you need further convincing, just compare the equipment mix at a trade show, like PRINT. Think back 10 years ago and recall all of the heavy iron that once dominated the show floor. Today, and for the past several shows, perhaps only a single offset press could be found on the trade show floor. Similarly, scan the pages of Printing Impressions magazine and see which industry suppliers are advertising. That should give you some clues as to future trends.

Get into digital, and now inkjet, printing because it's the right next step for your business. Get into it because your order sizes are shrinking and you realize that your clients need to be more nimble. Buy digital iron to give you job flexibility, personalization capabilities and faster turnaround times. The point is, "go digital" for the right reasons, at the right time, and after doing some research (like, um, reading a book on the subject, for example).

Finally, if you somehow still remain on the fence, just ask your customers where their business needs are headed. You are likely to hear phrases that connotate uncertainty and anxiety in their answers. They might know where they'd like to be in the months and years ahead, but realize that getting there could come down to be a matter of trial and error. As you read these pages, you will see that digital printing technology is designed to answer these needs, offering customers the option of trying out new marketing ideas, experiencing errors, making adjustments, and trying again.

And so, we begin...

Let's start with some realities and fundamentals that will form the basis of your success, while allowing the authors to display how wicked "smaht" they are so they can double their speaking fees.

If you have any questions or need clarification, please connect with one or both of us (especially if you need help training your salespeople). We'd be happy to be of assistance.

Bill Farquharson
bill@aspirefor.com
AspireFor.com
25BestSalesTips.com

Kelly Mallozzi
kelly@successinprint.net
www.successinprint.net

SECTION ONE

10 Digital Realities,
Fundamental Truths
& Key Concepts

Section One: 10 Digital Realities, Fundamental Truths & Key Concepts

Early adopters of digital printing learned some harsh lessons. Despite what the vendors claimed, we weren't in Kansas anymore. This wasn't going to be easy. Not at all. The typical mistake printers made was to treat digital like every other tool in their toolbox of output solutions. It was possible for them to say to customers, "Guess what? We now sell color copies!" and expect clients to understand what they were talking about. But "Guess what? Now we can print directly from your digital file!" was met with blank stares of confusion. Digital printing gave printers new capabilities and demanded a new approach.

Even the digital printing equipment vendors got it wrong. For example, one supplied their digital clients with banners that read, "If you can put it on a disk, we can print from it." The result? People came in with floppy disks containing files that consisted of single-page résumés, causing a disaster when their "simple" file wasn't formatted properly. Corrections took time and resulted in unbillable prepress charges. Then, once everything was all set to go, the digital output of 25 "copies" would ultimately turn into a sale that generated only a few dollars.

To say the least, some customer education about file submission was necessary, another first for the printing industry. It was going to take a new approach, one that was more tactical and anecdotal. What's more, printers would have to do something they'd never done before: Market themselves. In addition, the traditional Print Buyer was no longer the desired contact. Salespeople had to go deeper into their client's organization to find the Requisitioner (the originator of the document). This ripped sales reps out of their comfort zones, causing them to report, "No one buys digital print, boss" as a way of hiding their fear for this new technology and their ignorance/laziness/unwillingness to change.

The journey towards selling digital printing successfully and profitably, begins with the benefit of not being the first to have gone down this path. Here are 10 important lessons for you to learn:

#1 No untapped market

Those of us who have been around since the introduction of the digital press will remember that the equipment manufacturers promised us a mammoth and miraculous mass of clients who would be falling all over themselves to buy what we had to offer — if we would just buy their digital presses. Customers, we were told, were just waiting for the chance to denounce the evil paper master and readily embrace the electronic file.

What we learned early on was that it was all just a dream, a fictitious belief that someone in Marketing had conjured up, a best-case scenario that was never even close to reality. We bought into it, but when we bought it, customers did not come...at least not in droves. Some incremental new business did trickle in, but no one was getting rich quick and retiring in Fiji from the proceeds of all the digital printing sales they made. The only thing mammoth about digital printing was the amount of convincing it took for clients to "go digital" and place that first order without providing a paper master. But with it also came the first clue that this technology was a true game-changer and worth the effort: Once customers went digital and saw the benefits, they never went back to their old ways.

No, there is no untapped market for digital printing. Not then and not now. This is your first lesson to learn. The job of finding suitable applications and educating the market is yours if you are to be successful. And while here we are 25 years later and the digital press has become even more ubiquitous than it was 10 years ago, you must still sell the value and benefits of digital printing one customer at a time. We are no longer talking about digital printing as being a possibility. Rather, today it is a certainty and the conversations have become more about augmentation and integration. At least now there are success stories to tell.

In the end, Dale Carnegie had it right in his 1936 book, How to Win Friends and Influence People, when he said, "You can get what you want when you figure out what the other guy wants and help him to get it." Modernized and put into terms of this subject at hand, "You can realize profitability after you first understand a client's business needs, and then fulfill those needs through digital printing solutions."

#2 No quick, profitable, digital/inkjet/variable data printing sales

Everyone out there selling printing today knows all too well that gone are the days when it was possible to walk into someone's office for the first time and walk out with an order. Selling cycles just seem to be getting longer and longer. The second reality, then, is that there is no such thing as a quick, profitable digital printing sale. Sure, you'll make some quick sales, but they are likely to be won on the basis of price. And yes, profitable sales also exist, but they are going to require time, patience and a lot of customer education. If you are a sales rep, this should be the point where your ears perk up and you say, "Educate them? That sounds more like Marketing than it does Sales. Who's supposed to do that, me or my company?" DING-DING-DING! You are asking the right question. We'll talk more about that later.

The other force that delays the digital printing sale is simple fear. In general, customers hate change. Despite the fact that what they're doing might not be working, it's the way things have been done since the day the earth cooled. They're more inclined to go with the devil they know than to take a risk on something risky and unproven, like digital printing. Salespeople, you will experience frustration when you do an exhaustive search of a client's business needs and come up with a better print solution using digital/inkjet printing, only to have seemingly inane objections thrown at you. When this happens, understand that you are selling into a fearful environment.

Organizations also seem to involve more people in every decision they make now. Ask anyone who has gone on a job interview lately. Whereas 10 years ago a person might have gone on two or three interviews before getting a job offer, today it is not unusual to have to show up for six or more face-to-face, phone, and SKYPE interviews. When no one wants to have to take the blame for a "mistake," decisions can take forever. But you don't have forever to make your sales goal, do you? Just go down this road knowing that the success you seek is more likely to be over the horizon than it is around the corner. Profitable digital/inkjet printing sales are absolutely out there, but the seeds first need to be sewn, fertilized and harvested. As a result, set realistic expectations.

#3 Solve the problem, earn the order

Don't "sell" digital printing. Instead, earn a seat at the Cool Table by applying the right printing solution. Trust us, your boss does not need you to spend your time soliciting bids, looking for opportunities to provide pricing, and building a book of business that consists of low-profit orders from clients who will not show any loyalty. If that's his or her goal, an Internet-based campaign is all that's necessary.

Back when the two of us were selling print, it was perfectly acceptable to use a sales approach that consisted of some version of, "Can I provide you with some pricing?" Print opportunities were abundant. The economy was humming along. Selling solutions was an option, not a necessity. Sales success was possible without sales skills. Today, however, it is mandatory if you want to stay in this business. Print — digital or otherwise — will be seen as a gallon of milk and you will be subjected to bid after bid if you don't up your game when selling digital printing.

Where do these solutions come from? They are the result of a sales process whereby the sales rep does more than just learn the specifications of the job. Time is taken to understand what the customer is trying to accomplish — and even their overall business strategy — so an idea can be presented that either solves a problem or fills a need. The good news: It's fun! The better news is: It's profitable! The process of understanding what clients are all about and what they want to accomplish, and then choosing the correct tool in your toolbox of capabilities, is deeply rewarding. Oh, and you can make a lot of commission dollars in the process, too!

Later in this book we'll give you some specific vertical markets to target, along with suggestions for successfully creating digital printing opportunities for yourself and your company. For now, let's borrow one of those stories to help drill this point home:

> It's payday and you stroll into your bank's lobby, waiting in line for a teller to become available (you would just snap a picture and make the deposit via the mobile app, however, it's your commission check and, naturally, it exceeds the maximum amount allowed). Scanning the lobby, you notice a banner tacked to the wall that reads: "Refinance your car with us. 3.99% APR." From here, you've got two choices: Sell or Solve.

Sell: The sales-focused Print Sales Rep would seek out the person who buys that banner in an effort to provide pricing. While it's likely that the outcome will include the phrase "Your price is too high," if a sale is actually made, it will be only because all of the profit has been stripped away. The customer, in this case, is the only one who can claim victory.

Solve: The solutions-focused Print Sales Rep takes a different approach. Walking over to the Assistant Manager's desk, an attempt is made to learn about that particular promotion and who is in charge of it. Then, after depositing the commission check, the Problem Solver returns to his/her office and formulates a plan:

"I need to learn more about what the bank is trying to do, what success they've had so far, and what constitutes their target market. If I can accomplish that, perhaps I can come up with a print solution to help the bank make this promotion a big success."

So, armed with an opportunity and a name, the next step is to come up with a list of potential questions to ask that help uncover the bank's goals and marketing plan. At that point, you are ready to contact the Decision-Maker with a sales approach that sounds something like this:

> "I understand that you are in charge of the car refinancing promotion that I saw in your lobby. The purpose of my call is to discuss how I can help you make that promotion a success. The solutions that I provide include digital/inkjet and variable data printing. This gives you the option of segmenting markets and customizing messages. I'd like to learn more about what you are trying to achieve, what you've done so far, and the level of success you've had in the hopes that I can design an appropriate solution."

Solve the problem. Don't just sell digital printing. See the difference? When you approach a prospect, remember: The problem is not that they are spending too much on their print procurement.

The problem is... something else. Typically, every company or organization faces the challenge of revenue growth. Other than Mergers & Acquisitions, there are only three ways for businesses to grow their sales:

a. Find more customers;
b. Sell more to existing customers; or
c. Expand into new, profitable markets that serve a different target audience.

If you can help a company to solve one or all of these problems, you will earn orders at profitable levels. Instead of being brought in at the Quote stage of the job ("Can you give me a price on these specifications?"), you are now taking part in the Design stage. Here, the conversation is about meeting business needs and overcoming challenges, not just print specs. Which conversation would you rather be involved in? Which one do you think is going to lead to a more profitable and loyal customer?

What it takes to get there is an understanding that selling digital/inkjet printing will require you to conduct some research on the company prior to the start of the prospecting process, so that your sales approach is solutions-based. Much more on this later but the importance of this skill cannot be understated.

#4 Customer databases typically range from nonexistent to vastly inferior

One important and valuable outcome from marrying the digital printing press with the computer is variable data printing. This can mean a project is as complicated as highly targeted marketing or as "simple" as a basic mailing campaign. Either way, there is something you need to understand about the customer's data: It sucks. It's crap. It's inaccurate. It's yours to fix. That said, it's an opportunity, too.

More than likely, there is also no one single file that contains all of the data. You are destined to receive multiple files in different programs (programs that don't talk to each other, by the way), and even if there is one list, it is far from accurate. What's more, there's no single individual who knows where all of the records are kept. The point is, you must go into each selling situation with the assumption that time will be spent consolidating and correcting the customer's mailing list, if it exists at all.

Weeeeeeeeeeee! Are we having fun yet?

This digital reality comes into play especially when you are looking at variable data printing software. Before you leap, part of your due diligence must be to look into the effort around cleaning up customer databases. Remember: garbage in, garbage out.
to repeat. It's not that you are disloyal (though the Vice President of Marketing at Wellesley Bank in my home state of Massachusetts told me 80% of customers hate their bank!), it's just most of us are locked in to our current bank out of sheer, well, laziness, I suppose. You are loyal to your existing bank in a way that's similar to how our customers look at us if they are tied in electronically: Leaving would be painful to them.

The lesson here: Get people connected with you electronically as fast as possible.

#5 DP is like Vitamin E

If you research the origin of vitamin E, you'll find a somewhat boring and scientific account of its discovery ... except for one thing. When Vitamin E was invented, scientists had no idea what it did. That is, they knew it solved a problem, but which problem was unclear. For a while, they called it a "cure looking for a disease."

This is a pretty good analogy for the early days of digital printing. For example, when the black-and-white Xerox DocuTech became available, its intended use was for in-plant printing operations. Imagine Xerox's surprise, then, when quick and small commercial printers started buying multiple devices and cranking out hundreds of thousands, and even millions, of clicks per month. Similar to Vitamin E, the early market for digital printing was misunderstood at the onset.

One constant over time: The only people who care about digital printing equipment's speeds and feeds are printers. What customers care about is how the technology can solve their problems and meet their business needs. That's where the focus needs to be, regardless of whether you are in sales or management. Instead of talking about why digital printing is great and why your customer just MUST take advantage of it, it's better to talk about applications. What are some real-world examples of ways that digital printing has been used effectively in ways that offset just couldn't replicate?

Digital printing solves problems. Since its inception, it has solved many. And being a problem-solver is your magical wand of differentiation. Instead of calling up and asking to speak to the individual who buys the print, YOU are the day-saver— you and your great ideas.

Digital printing helps creative people be creative. You'll find that, when presented correctly, months will pass between your presentation and the actual sale, in part because you've planted a seed, giving clients new capabilities (a cure). And it might take a long time before that cure finds the right application (the disease). Our prediction: Your phone will ring, and it will be a prospect you called on 6-12 months ago. After getting over the shock of hearing from them, you hear them say, "Do you remember telling me about the capabilities of that that new digital/inkjet equipment?

Well, I was in a meeting this morning and my boss was lamenting how we need to send out just one marketing message, instead of testing several. I thought of you." If, and when, that scenario ever happens, just remember that we told you so.

Side story:

Many moons ago, I (Bill) was doing a private gig for F.P. Horak in Bay City, Michigan. The event was held in a planetarium, thus providing comical acoustics. The audience was made up of creatives, graphic designers, and ad agency and marketing types. Talking up the many applications enabled by digital print, I told story after story, holding up samples as I went. As I looked out over the audience, I started to notice that very few were maintaining eye contact with me. Most were leaning back and staring straight up at the ceiling. I was certain that my presentation was a complete disaster and I remember racing out of there for fear that Tim Dust, the guy who hired me, would want his money back. A few weeks later in New York City, I was at a trade show and Tim called out my name as he walked over to me. I was horrified and certain that he was going to tell me what a terrible job I did. When I confessed my fear to him, Tim laughed and said, "Bill, those people weren't ignoring you. They were personalizing all the stories you related to them. Our phone has been ringing off the hook ever since you left." Looks like vitamin E cures a problem after all!

#6 New definition of loyal

A fairy tale: Once upon a time, in a land far, far away, there was a phenomenon called The Loyal Customer. Here, a client was most likely to stick with its incumbent printer and the account was serviced by a single sales rep for years, sometimes even decades. Pricing was important but was by no means the king of this land. Occasionally, there were problems and errors, but so strong was the bond between customer and vendor that small bumps in the road were overlooked and, as the sun set, they held hands and gazed into each other's eyes.

But then, times changed. Customers became much savvier. Printers decided that lowering prices was the best way to improve sales. Competition became rampant; even the UPS drop-off spot started selling print. Chaos ensued and fights between clients and printers broke out, forever destroying their kinship and making customers only as loyal as the last job they received. The spell had been broken. Until one day...Digital print was discovered, loyalty was restored, and there was joy throughout the land. The end.

Back then, customer loyalty was tied to personal relationships, good service, and a history of working together. Oh, and money. You see, another factor that made it hard for companies to switch printers easily was the fact that jobs were printed using film and plates at a cost that, once paid for on the first job, gave the incumbent printer a built-in competitive advantage over any fellow printers that sought to knock them off the throne. Customers were loyal because it was in their best financial interest to remain so.

But technology advancement changed everything. Digital printing, along with the emergence of the Internet, made the entire print production process a lot less personal. Now, a person with virtually no graphic design experience can log onto an online storefront, create a piece (that may even be personalized), and have it printed without having to talk directly to anyone. And, depending on the printing organization, there is a good chance that no human hands will touch that customer file at all. An automated workflow will take that job all the way through the production process. The only people to see it will be a press operator and perhaps a quality control person, if the client is lucky. Repeat orders, then, become less about who owns the plates and more about who owns the Web-to-print interface, the digital files, and the order entry information. Because of the complexity of a digitally-produced piece (especially if variable data is incorporated), the vendor that houses and maintains a customer's data has a virtually unbreakable hold on that client. Think about your own experience on Amazon. It's possible to reorder, say, guitar strings, without ever having put the guitar down. Your information is already there, and the reorder comes down to:

- Stop strumming
- Log in
- Swipe
- Swipe
- Select
- Enter order
- Resume strumming

Do you want to reestablish the concept of customer loyalty? Remember the new definition of loyalty:

a. It's the file!
b. It's the file!
c. It's the file!

#7 Your salespeople won't/don't care

How's that for a headline? Just what you wanted to hear if you're an owner or company president who is considering taking the plunge into digital printing. If that's you and you are reading those words, how did that news hit you? After doing all that work and spending all that money, two consultants from New England have the nerve to contend that the salespeople you employ, the same ones you are counting on—nay, assumed would share your passion and enthusiasm—Couldn't. Care. Less.

Okay, now that we have that all settled, we can move on....

Wait. Are you not onboard with that point? What? You've never even considered the possibility? Well then, let's back up and prove it to you.

Imagine that you are a printing rep sitting in a sales meeting. It's a hastily-arranged get-together and the rumor is that a new piece of equipment has been purchased and will be installed soon. The owner enters the room, and everyone finds their chairs. With a big smile on his face, he says,

> *"Ladies and gentlemen, it is with great pleasure that I announce our entry into the world of digital/variable data printing. I recently signed the papers for a new Xerindigo-Canorinolta 25000 and I wanted to tell you myself so that you can start preparing your sales approach."*

The salespeople stir, giving each other suspicious looks as the owner continues:

> *"I'll spare you the details about speeds and feeds because, quite frankly, I've forgotten every-thing except for the price* <<insert *polite laughter here>>. What this means for you is the following:*
> - *Selling digital/inkjet printing is a complicated sale. It's new and highly technical for many of you. Therefore, you'll be selling a product that you do not fully understand and very well may feel stupid;*
> - *You will also be approaching a different kind of customer, someone who is more technically profi-*

cient, marketing-results driven, and might as well speak an entirely different language. Gone are the days when you spend time dealing with traditional Print Buyers. Now, you will need to collaborate with technical/IT people and marketing types, moving you way out of your comfort zone. So, you'll likely be lost;

- *The orders that you pursue will be a lot smaller than you are used to. Subsequently, the commissions you'll receive will be minuscule by comparison. And, thus, you'll feel cheated;*
- *It's going to be a much longer selling cycle when selling digital/inkjet printing. Um, you'll get impatient;*
- *So, you can expect to be frustrated every step of the way, working longer and harder — all so that you can make less money than you're accustomed to in the past.*

"Okay," bellows the print shop owner, *"who's with me????"* <<sound: crickets>>

Can you understand the sales staff's hesitation? This is a problem we will solve in these pages. For now, be aware of the new digital/inkjet printing sales process. And when you are done crying and gnashing your teeth in a biblical manner, move on to the next point, which is...

#8 The selling cycle can be double that of traditional print

(Boy, the news just gets better and better, doesn't it?)

We talked a little bit in #2 about how there is no quick digital/

inkjet sale. Today, it is impossible to predict an average selling cycle (the time between initial customer contact and that first order) when it comes to digital/inkjet, but suffice it to say that it's not the usual 3- to 6-month period found with traditional commercial printing sales. The entire point is that we are trying to use digital output to disrupt an organization's current process. And disruption is, well, disruptive. Words like "change" and "new" can be extremely unsettling to salespeople for whom the concept is unfamiliar (Duh!) and so our challenge becomes making them feel comfortable being uncomfortable. Sounds tough, right?

Yes and no. If you know that you are dealing with a traditionalist who does not like change and you do the work up front to make your case, educate, and dedicate yourself to making that person GET comfortable, the process will go a lot smoother. Ignore those additional steps, however, and you can measure the selling cycle in terms of decades. This is done by removing as much of the fear away as possible. You do it by keeping the sales rep's ego intact. You do it with sales training, resources, and leaning on the vendors who sold you that big beautiful gray box for market development support materials. You do it by locking everyone – vendors and salespeople and marketing managers (if you have them) — in a room and saying, "I will not let you out of here until you are all whistling zippadeedoodah and feeling good about our digital/inkjet capabilities."

We are kind of kidding, but only kind of. No one wants to feel dumb. Do not make your salespeople feel dumb. Assure them you are with them every step of the way and that you will provide everything they need to be successful. If you're the owner, lead by example. Learn how to sell digital/inkjet printing yourself. Make sales calls yourself. Don't ask anyone on your team to do something you, yourself, are not willing or able to do.

As we say about a lot of things in sales, the first time you do it is always the hardest. After you have gained some success in helping clients and prospects embrace the concept of digital/inkjet printing — often tied into data-driven marketing campaigns — you will get better and better at selling the benefits and value proposition. Eventually, the concepts will become part of your daily sales process. It will become who you are and what you do.

And here's the ironic part: One of the biggest selling features of digital/inkjet printing is being quicker to market, more flexible, enabling variable data, and adopting more of a just-in-time mindset. So, it may seem counter-intuitive that your message is about being nimble, while you witness prospects and clients dragging their feet. So, shine a spotlight on it. Face any discomfort and hesitation they may have head on. Be anecdotal and show the client how others have successfully implemented similar solutions. Make sure that your sales message is infused with language that is all about movement, action and results.

Your enthusiasm, and the case history examples that you present about what happens to companies once they adopt a similar on-demand, just-in-time mindset, will rub off on them. The benefits of digital/inkjet are so exciting. And your language and manner of enthusiasm should be, too.

#9 Key Concept: The 10/1/ Ratio

When Bill started his first job out of college, one of the first lessons in his sales training class formed the cornerstone of UARCO Business Forms' sales philosophy. It had to do with the relationship between the price of the printed piece ($1) and the cost of using it ($20). What shows up on the Purchase Order reflects only what a company spends on the specifications of the job—quantity, inks, paper, finishing, etc. This becomes the focus for every typical print—or, in this case, digital print—salesperson. Their thinking is, "I can provide lower pricing and, therefore, win the business." There are many problems with this approach, but here are two of the more important ones: First of all, there is no infusion of or reason for building customer loyalty. If you win a job on price, you can just as easily lose the next one on price as well. Second, there is no profit in selling print at poor or nonexistent margins Other than that, go for it!

It's only when you focus on the usage cost of the document that you can understand the true value of digital/inkjet printing. Digital output is very rarely less expensive than traditional commercial printing. More often than not, the order runs are smaller, which makes the price per thousand higher for digital, thus making it impossible to show the value in hard dollars. But, by learning how a solution that involves digital/inkjet printing saves the customer money by lowering that usage cost—giving them options they've never had before—or increases the value of the document, the sales rep can demonstrate where digital/inkjet printing fits and justify the (likely) higher price.

By definition, the 20/1 Ratio states that for every dollar the client spends on any given printed piece, they spend an average of $20 using it. That "$20 area" can include waste and obsolescence, warehousing and labor, etc. Essentially, all costs associated with that piece, from the time it arrives in receiving to the time that it is shipped out with a product or discarded, are considered to be "the usage cost."

Why is this important?

This concept is necessary as a way of explaining the need for a digital/inkjet printing solution. It's easy for the client to understand the "$1 area." It's the number that appears after the word "Total" on the Purchase Order. Duh! That makes it tangible. But no one ever thinks about the other side of the equation, which becomes one of the primary jobs for the digital printing sales rep.

It's critical to convey this difference and to get the customer to understand that they will save money well beyond just the purchase price.

This example might help (true story, by the way)...

A company based in Chicago put its Sell Sheets out to bid, soliciting prices from five different printers. Four of the printers gave the specifications to their Estimator and then stood by, tapping their feet, while they waited for a price quote so that they could deliver the proposal to the Buyer.

The salesperson at the fifth printer took a different approach. She called the Buyer and asked permission to do some research. Her goal was to find out how the Sell Sheets were being used. In other words, she wanted to look into the "$20 area." After some convincing, the Buyer granted the request and gave her access to the various people involved.

First, she went to the head of Marketing and was told that Sell Sheets were used as leave-behinds by the company's salespeople all across the country. Next, she did some research on LinkedIn and found the name of one of the company's sales reps. Via email, she learned that the reps all worked from home offices and sent in periodic requests for the Sell Sheets, depending on their current inventory and need.

So far, nothing interesting or unusual here.

On a whim, she wandered down to the company's Shipping & Receiving department, frustrated and running out of time and questions, since the pricing was due the next day. The crew was at break and she found them sitting on boxes and pallets enjoying their morning coffee. Introducing herself and quickly summarizing what she was doing, she asked them what she thought was a pretty stupid question: "Is there anything unusual about these Sell Sheets?" and received an odd response:

"Other than the fact that the salespeople are idiots? No, not really," one worker replied.

Such a strange answer demanded further explanation. But before she could say anything, another worker added, "Yup! If it weren't for their procrastination and laziness, I probably wouldn't have a job." That answer intrigued her even more and the look on her face was taken as an invitation to explain.

"You see," said the worker, "the salespeople use these Sell Sheets in their presentations and for trade shows. However, they always wait until the last minute before reordering from our inventory and, as a result, we have to ship them using one overnight service or another. I'm usually the one who does that, and some days it can take me two or three hours to open the boxes, grab what is needed, package and ship the materials. It wastes a lot of my time."

Money is being wasted, too, thought the printing sales rep. "How much money in overnight shipping costs would you estimate is spent sending these Sell Sheets to the salespeople?" she asked. At this point, everyone turned to the boss, who made a face and then answered, "As much as $1,000 a month during the busy season, plus the cost of my laborer."

Thanking the crew profusely, she left the building and returned to her car. When she got there, she reconnected with the company salesperson to seek confirmation. A response came back almost immediately that validated what she had learned.

Returning to the office, the print sales rep did some more research and found a list of sales offices on the company's website. As expected, they were all located in major cities across the country.

By the end of the next day, the Buyer had four proposals for the Sell Sheets as indicated in the bid and one proposal that detailed a new idea for the way the Sell Sheets could be produced: Instead of printing locally and shipping nationally, the proposal indicated that the orders would be fulfilled regionally—at printing facilities around the country—and shipped out locally.

At no charge.

The print sales rep would later explain that the Sell Sheets would be produced on-demand on digital/inkjet printers. Not only would this eliminate the shipping costs (which the Buyer later estimated at close to $8,000 a year), it would give the Marketing Department the flexibility to change their messaging, print different versions, and even customize the Sell Sheets for specific trade shows and conferences.

Not surprisingly, she was awarded the business...at nearly twice the price of the highest competitive bid from the other four printers!

Had she focused on the per piece purchase price of the document, the print sales rep would have competed apples for apples. But, by learning the story behind the printed piece and coming up with a better solution, she earned an order at her pricing level and differentiated herself to the point where she was asked to come in and do similar analysis on a variety of the customer's other printed products.

The end.

Again, understanding the 20/1 ratio can be the difference between winning a job based on a low price and earning an order based on providing a better solution. Everyone focuses on the purchase price of the document. Learn to ask questions that uncover its usage costs.

- "What is the purpose of this piece?"
- "How many get thrown out?"
- "How often does it change?"
- "Do you see a value in ordering only what you need in the short-term?"

Your ability to master this sales skill will help you sell not just digital/inkjet printing more profitably, but every product and value-added service that you offer. It's that important.

#10 Hard work is up front

Do you remember how we told you a couple of "realities" ago that industry salespeople are not overly interested in selling digital/inkjet printing? One of the bullet point reasons was that the orders, and therefore the commissions, are low. It's easy to see why this could be a deterrent.

What printing salespeople need to understand is that if their effort occurs almost exclusively at the beginning of the sale, the amount of time that they spend dealing with that order afterward will be virtually eliminated. Put anecdotally, it's like convincing a customer to let you hook up the hose to the side of their building so that all of the printed matter can be transferred to you. The sales rep does the convincing, but quickly steps aside so that the technical people can do their thing. Once that hose is connected securely and jobs flow freely, very often the first time a sales rep hears about an individual order is when the commission shows up on his or her paycheck. Sure, the dollar amount might not be that of a traditional, longer-run print job, but the checks come more frequently and they cash just the same, thankyouverymuch.

SECTION TWO

Common Denominators Among
the Successful/Profitable

Section Two:
Common Denominators Among the Successful/Profitable

At this point in the book, having had your assumptions challenged and your world rocked a bit by two Cliff Clavin-type (remember him, the know-it-all from Cheers?) authors, you could be feeling everything from excitement to nausea. There's a lot that happens in the real world that doesn't show up in an equipment brochure or promotional video. It might not be the news you wanted to hear but, unless you heat your house by burning $100 bills, you need to hear it if your goal is to become successful at selling digital/inkjet printing.

The good news is that we are done discussing the negative and will now happily regale you with stories, examples, and factors that make the best of the best, the best of the best. Again, success leaves clues and breadcrumbs for others to follow. If you currently offer digital/inkjet printing, here are some ideas for getting to the next level. If your print shop is still on the fence, use the following points to do the adoption process right, starting with a point that serves as a core belief among the profitable.

1. Technically Superior

It's not an accident that the first subject discussed under the heading of "common denominators among the successful/profitable" is the ability to be technically superior to your competition. This is a critical point to understand as it underscores one of the major differences in digital/inkjet printing technology versus anything else the graphic arts industry has ever seen.

With all due respect to the equipment manufacturers that might hire us in the future, we offer the following...

Once upon a time it might have been important for you to have more equipment firepower or quicker response times than your competition. The iron you had on the floor that made up your equipment list defined your company, served as an important differentiator, and was the focal point of your sales presentations. Today, yes, the equipment still matters. The fact that your digital device cranks out terrific quality, at high speeds, is important, but it's not the key to your success. Unless you have rewired the engine, tricking it out with unique capabilities, here's what your customer base needs to know about your digital/inkjet press:

It's beige and it uses electricity.

Far more important than the output device is your technical ability, workflow automation and capabilities on the front end. Do you have Jedi-level knowledge of all major software programs? Can clients not only enter orders electronically via a Web interface, but also check order status? Your prepress department should be second to none in capabilities and skills. In fact, one of the goals of your company should be to gain a reputation for expertise in this area. It's what you'll want to talk about when the time comes to do some marketing (discussed in a few pages).

This "Technically Superior" point first became evident to Bill when he interviewed an early adopter (circa 1995) of digital print in the Boston area, a company called Will/Land Printing (now a part of Flagship Press). Debbie Riccio, the co-owner and top salesperson, graciously gave him an hour of her time so that he could learn the keys to her company's early success. At the time, Bill was a print broker and Will/Land was his vendor of choice.

He knew first-hand how good they were and Deb was pulling back the curtain so that he could understand why they were also a profit leader. Their production capabilities included Xerox Docu-Tech black-and-white digital printers, but they had nowhere near the firepower of some competitors in the area (King Printing, a local competitor, had 14 DocuTechs and was seemingly feeding entire forests directly into them). Deb's company couldn't keep up with King's output abilities, nor was she even interested in the low-profit, high-volume sale.

Instead, it was Will/Land's technical superiority that kept her phone ringing. Their typical customer was not someone who needed a quote on thousands of books and software manuals; but rather it was individuals who were encountering file problems, and Deb welcomed them all. Her technical staff fixed the issues and educated the clients on how to make print-ready files that were maximized for Will/Land's digital equipment. Subsequently, customers not only stayed loyal (because they didn't have to go through the process all again with a new vendor), they often didn't even ask for a price. Such was the value of being Technically Superior.

In fact, after the interview, Deb's assistant handed her three phone messages that had come in while she was talking to Bill. Each carried the same theme: "You helped an associate of mine with a software problem and I've got something similar. I hear you are expert at dealing with problem files. Please call me." That is the type of brand you'll strive toward, too, if you want to beat price objections by avoiding them altogether.

The last piece of the Technically Superior goal is the print salesperson. By no means do you need or even want your reps to be experts, and you certainly will not want them involved with file manipulation. But they should be armed with some basic information and they should be able to answer some of the more simpler questions that a prospect or client might ask. Making a "cheat sheet" available to the sales team will head off a lot of problems. Remember: Salespeople typically offer up a "Yes, we can absolutely do that!" knee-jerk response and then figure out how to do it later (or pass it off to someone else and make it their problem). Teach the reps which programs are supported, some basic questions to ask regarding the files themselves, and when it's necessary to bring in the cavalry.

Summary: How to become technically superior:

1. Recognize that while the output equipment choice is important, it's not your lead sled dog. Prepress is;
2. Hire the best, most technically capable prepress personnel you can find/afford;
3. Train them on the most popular software programs and automated digital workflows until they are Ninja, Jedi, Bill Gates-level subject matter experts;
4. Teach the salespeople what they need to know, including answers to some common questions, and make them aware of the software programs your company excels in;
5. Market a "we're all that and a bag of chips" technically superior message.

2. The Right Staff

Two printing companies "go digital." One has wild success. The other, not so much. With similar iron on the floor, you'd have to look elsewhere to determine why there is a difference. One area to focus on would be personnel. There are several specific points where it is imperative to have the right bodies placed, namely:

A Technical Communicator

Do you remember us talking about how important it is to be technically superior? We sure hope so because it was, like, two pages ago. Someone has to be the point person for this nomenclature. Who's it going to be? You? No. You need a Technical Communicator.

Think about that job title for a second —Technical Communicator: a tech-savvy soul with the gift of gab. It's an almost unimaginable combo platter of skills and personality. Yet without one on staff, you'd better be servicing a client base that submits perfect files every time. No? Then let's break that down...

- First, consider the common personality traits of the highly technical data management, IT programming and postal optimization experts that you know. Not exactly the kind of person you'd want to get stuck next to on an airplane while flying a long distance, that is, unless your goal is to learn about the fascinating world of binary depolarization. While brilliant in their own field, their commitment to interpersonal skills is often lacking.

- Next, consider the communicator. Images of Ronald Reagan, Tony Robbins, or Oprah Winfrey might come to mind. Their "superpower" has to do with the transfer of information in a way that is clear, easy to understand, and frequently quite motivating. Typically, the personality of the Communicator is described using words like, "gregarious," "amiable," "outgoing," and "engaging." "Tech-savvy" does not generally make that list.

- Now, put those two people together in a Panini-maker and you have someone with unmatched abilities to manipulate different files, who knows the ins and outs of data transfer, plus has the ability to easily explain intricate "how to" details to a client. Do you know many people who fit that description? We didn't think so. It's rare. Not impossible to find, but definitely rare.

Why is it critical to have a Technical Communicator on staff? Lots of reasons:

1. The majority of first-time customers still submit faulty files;
2. Your goal is to be technically superior to the competition, remember? And...
3. Your marketing efforts will be a lot more effective if you can boast about your shop's abilities to solve technical challenges.

Printing the job on a digital device is the last step in a complicated process and, by comparison, the easiest. A lot of hard work went into prepress and file prep. What's left is the push of a button. This is a sharp contrast to the printing process of years ago, when a lot was riding on the skill set of the press operator. Today, a disproportionate chunk of a company's success in digital/inkjet printing falls on the shoulders of the Technical Communicator, such as:

- The ability to educate the sales force on the basics of digital/inkjet, the questions to ask, the types of customer files to they can expect, and some likely problems;
- Trusted enough to go on four-legged sales calls with the reps, meet with prospects and customers, communicate the file transfer process, workflow procedures, and the technical aspects of digital/inkjet printing;
- Can create technical guidelines to be displayed on the website, given to salespeople, and shared with customers with the goal of receiving print-ready jobs;
- Can lead client educational events such as webinars,

seminars, and open house demonstrations.
- Must keep up with trends and industry best practices.

Now, can you see why the Technical Communicator is so important? In fact, so valuable is this person that...wait...
<<STOP!!!!>>
(If you are the owner or company president, we strongly suggest that you redact or even tear out this entire page so that your Technical Communicator does not see how this sentence ends. Here goes...)

In fact, so valuable that they should be paid whatever they ask. (We warned you!). The Technical Communicator is the single most important person in a successful digital/inkjet print shop!

As far as finding someone who fits the job description of having superior technical skills coupled with superior communication skills, good luck. You'll find people with one or the other, but very rarely will you come across someone who possesses both traits. Your best bet is to start by finding a good communicator. It's a lot easier to teach technical skills than it is to teach personality.

Kelly provides her 2 cents here – You could also take a great desktop operator that has a glimmer of personality and cultivate the people skills part of this equation. One idea might be to put him/her through the sales training process and make sure the person understands the basics of engaging behavior and persuasive communication. Also teach him/her more about the customers themselves and WHY they use the solutions that they do. Think of it as a sales and marketing boot camp that you are willing to invest in to produce the kind of talent that is vital to your success. And then remember what we said before. Treat and pay him/her well.

Marketing Director (+ Lead Generator)

Marketing is a funny subject when it comes to the Graphics Arts. Printers have never had to do it before now. Isn't it enough just to have a sales force? Suddenly, it is a necessity, there are more medium options than ever, and there is more to talk about. A lot more. Oh, and the conversation now goes both ways, as there are customer reviews and feedback to consider. Printers know they need to market their wares but very few have a strategy other than a website and perhaps a Facebook page. If that. As for the message itself, it's no longer acceptable to define a printer by its equipment list. With digital/inkjet printing, a different tack must be taken. Now, stories must be told. Enter the Marketing Director.

Marketing is best thought of as stocking the pond with fish. It's getting the phone to ring, as well as identifying opportunities, applications, vertical markets, and—through lead generation—specific companies to call on. The best of the best understand that and have someone in the Marketing Director position. Some stop there while others take it farther and add the research piece for the salesperson: providing contact names, telephone numbers, email and LinkedIn addresses, as well as summaries created after website reviews. Couple that information with knowledge on how to sell to that particular vertical and the salesperson has an excellent chance of making a profitable sale. We'll talk about what this staff member should be doing a little later. For now, get the Help Wanted ad together and start looking for a Marketing Director.

Educated, Trained, Motivated Sales Force

Got five or more sales reps? Here's our prediction: You're going to have that one rep who just gets excited about absolutely everything. He/she is going to jump up and down and talk about how jazzed he/she is to get out there and start killing it. That sales rep will fully embrace digital/inkjet, see the opportunity, and engage with new and existing accounts, building a base of annuities just as you hoped would happen with all of the reps. Everyone else will want to kill him/her. The other reps will show as much interest in selling digital/inkjet as Americans do with watching professional soccer. For a number of reasons, we will cover later, they just don't care.

But, seriously, it is imperative that you have at least one go-getter, a sales rep who brings the right attitude to the challenge of digital/inkjet printing sales. At least then you can harness that energy and use him/her as the carrot AND the stick to beat everyone else into submission. There is no greater motivator to get the sales force going than watching this digital/inkjet sales innovator climb the sales ladder on the basis of sales. Suddenly, all of those arguments—orders/commissions are too small, new contact point at client, strange/confusing technology, long selling cycle—fade away. That's because sales reps think with their wallet. And, they are competitive as hell. No one wants to be made to look bad by their enthusiastic peer. Nope. Humiliation and ego are your friends here. Remember that point when it comes to compensation. For now, the challenge is to build a formidable sales force, starting with just one person if you must.

Thinking about what makes up the characteristics of a digital/inkjet printing sales rep? Look for qualities like creative, curious, and problem-solver. Digital/inkjet printing applications do not have little red flags on them. They are often hidden in plain sight, either currently being produced on an offset press or existing in the form of a problem waiting to be solved. You want a sales rep who is going to learn the story behind the printed piece and apply the digital/inkjet print solution when and where it fits. The first step in this process is to investigate and ask questions at a level that would make Lieutenant Columbo proud. That is, understand what it is the customer or prospect is trying to accomplish. This might mean speaking to multiple people in multiple departments, drilling down on a subject to a level that most print salespeople never get near. Consultative, solutions-based selling was once an option. Now, it's mandatory.

The obvious question is whether to use the existing sales force or to bring in someone new. Similar to our discussion regarding finding that Technical Communicator and starting with the personality you desire, can sales creativity be taught? Probably not, but management can teach applications and provide leads, essentially putting the ball on a tee and handing the rep a club. Finally—and we admit this might sound self-serving coming from two sales trainers—but just know that a major commitment to training must be made and maintained. In the beginning, it's about the basics. Later, it's all about applications in vertical markets. Kind of like this book, come to think of it!

Convert an existing sales rep, hire someone from the outside, or even think about moving up a CSR or Technical/Prepress specialist into the role; but just know that an educated, trained, and motivated sales force can make all the difference.

A Marketing Plan

Printers are notoriously bad at marketing themselves. If you're scoring at home, we've said that three times now. Just ask your salespeople. They have been complaining about getting a better brochure, or even a brochure at ALL, since the mid '90s. They cry that your website is an embarrassment and they are probably right. As an industry, we sell marketing solutions but do precious little for our own benefit. But given the fact that you have spent, or are seriously planning to invest, a bunch of money in digital/inkjet printing capacity, let's get the word out there, shall we? Good marketing is all about education. There are two levels to consider: Company and Personal (personal to the sales rep, that is). Ideally, the company delivers a consistent message and builds a brand.

If the company isn't doing any marketing (and gosh, what are the odds of that?), then it is up to the sales rep to fend for him/herself. This can mean an approach similar to what we suggest is done on a company level, only it will likely be a smaller and almost certainly less polished level. Either way, there are two parts to marketing—the message and the medium.

The Message

What do you want your potential clients to know about digital/inkjet? Puh-leaze don't think for a second they care about the make and model of your digital equipment or its speeds and feeds. Put yourself in their shoes and apply some Dale Carnegie thinking (Review: you can get what you want when you figure out what the other guy wants and help him to get it). What are the problems and challenges your target market faces? Crack that nut and your phone will ring.

We advise you to hit three separate points in your marketing message:

- Ease of doing business: We are technically superior to the competition;
- Success stories: Look at the great things we've done for others;
- Anecdotes and examples: If you are experiencing these problems or needs, we have your solution.

Ease of doing business with us

Here, the task is simple. Let prospective clients know that you are easy to work with. In fact, from file entry to communication, your message must be that you are "Amazon-easy" to work with. What's that? Like it or not, we live in an Amazon world. Amazon changed everything when Prime took off. Think about it: When you order something elsewhere and they don't offer free delivery in two days, what's your reaction? Us, too. We now expect Prime-like benefits from everyone. Is it fair? Of course not. But that's our new normal.

Online ordering and reordering are no longer a purple cow (an anomaly. Special. Unique. See Seth Godin's book by the same name to understand cleverness of authors' reference). Now, it's a global expectation. Personal interaction is nice, but it slows things down. Millennials, especially, want everything fast and instant. Give it to them.

Finally, it's all about constant and precise communication. Ideally, a client can click on a link and learn the exact location of their job (or at least an update on delivery). More likely, you are feeding them information proactively to ward off the, "Dude, where's my job?" phone call.

The bottom line is, customers need to know that digital/inkjet printing is a part of a greater experience that brings print into the 21st century of customer purchasing and information.

Sucess Stories

It cannot be overstated how important it is to understand that storytelling is a big part of marketing and selling digital/inkjet printing, perhaps more than any other form of graphic arts. Personify and demonstrate the value of digital/inkjet through stories. Having given countless presentations on digital/inkjet, we see light bulbs illuminate over the heads of our audience when we start spinning tales of applications we've seen or heard about. We're drifting into "The Medium" here but imagine a YouTube video that tells the story of challenges your client faced and how your digital/inkjet print solution solved them. A prospect watches that clip with interest since she faces a similar challenge. Your company's successful handling of the situation immediately depicts you as a problem-solver; creative, and different from the others. Successful marketing happens when the client calls you and says, "I watched your video and have a similar challenge. Can we talk?" Yahtzee!

Anecdotes and Examples

The client is trying to meet a specific business need or generate revenue and needs to know about the unique capabilities digital/inkjet provides. Picture a conference room filled with execs and whiteboards, blue-skying and spit-balling and whatever else those people do in order to think a problem through. They need to know you understand the challenges they are facing and that you've already solved similar ones for someone else. A marketing message that says, "Look what we've done for others," builds a solutions-based brand and will attract clients who want your help and your ideas, not just a bid.

The Mediums

Like a company that uses TV, radio, internet, and print to broadcast its message, you must reach your audience using a variety of mediums. Here are a few options:

Social Media

Most of the thought leaders in our industry agree that, at the bare minimum, you should be using YouTube, Twitter, LinkedIn, and Facebook on a regular basis. From there you can look at Instagram and Pinterest as platforms upon which you can cultivate a following of prospects who could become customers. The first advice we would give you is to check out your closest competition and see how they are using social media. Also check out your vendors to see if they have any stock material they can send you. When you're doing it yourself, social media does not cost you anything but time. Not using it is like ignoring a useful tool in your toolbox that COULD help you build your business.

For example, putting together a YouTube video like the one described previously is simple. That's not to say that you can't make it complicated, but it could be as simple as creating a PowerPoint presentation with four slides (or, if you're cool like us, use Keynote on your unnecessarily expensive Apple device);

Slide #1: Describe the problem you solved

Slide #2: Detail your brilliant solution

Slide #3: Explain the outcome

Slide #4: Give information about your company

In its simplest form, this could be nothing more than a voiceover, either scripted or a freestyle commentary. Don't be afraid to be folksy. Your video will not be in the running for a Golden Globe award anytime soon. The point is that you want to get the message across: If you've got this problem, we've got the solution and have solved it for someone else. This sets you up as a solutions provider and a subject matter expert. It also differentiates you immediately.

Once the YouTube video is completed, you can post the link on LinkedIn, Twitter, etc., as well as add the URL to the signature line of your emails.

Before you dismiss the idea of producing a YouTube video as too complicated or not worth your time, know this...

Bill was once hired to produce five YouTube promotional videos for a printer. After two, the owner decided they weren't worth the money and the gig ended despite Bill's plea to give it time and the prediction it would pull in leads as promised. Two years passed, and the owner called out of the blue to sheepishly admit that each video had received thousands of hits and several incoming calls a month as a result.

Are they difficult to produce? No. Do they work? Yes. Free? They can be. Worth it? Oh, yes. Most definitely.

The truth is, using social media (and blogging for that matter) can often feel like shouting into the abyss. Without comments, likes and shares, you have no idea if people are reading your stuff and what they are thinking. But here's the truth: You NOT being on social media says something too. It says that you are not interested in keeping up with the times, and that you are not innovating. Please don't let people say that about you. Assume they are watching, reading, and picking up what you are putting down. Validation comes when you get a call many months after a video is originally posted. The caller says some form of, "I was in a meeting today and remembered the video I saw posted on your website months ago. You might be able to help us."

View YouTube as a sales pitch. Add new stories and testimonials as frequently as you can. Give your digital/inkjet offerings that five-star-rating coveted by Amazon sellers. It's your 24/7 sales force, one that never complains.

As this is not a tutorial on the differences between LinkedIn, Twitter, Facebook, and the other forms of social media, let's just say we encourage you to build a network on each, perhaps setting a goal of 10 new followers a week. Then, set a goal for posting new messages and links, and stick with it. For example, you can just re-tweet once a day, put up one post to Facebook once a week, and post one article up onto LinkedIn each week. We'll sum up the subject of social media as a marketing medium like this: Tell the story on YouTube. Share the story on everything else.

Content Creation

Videos are just one form of content—a way to share anecdotes and successes. There are others:

1. *White Paper*

    Think of these as "How-to" reports. Consider the problems your digital/inkjet device solves and then write about it. For example, a White Paper with the title, "Five Ways to Make the Most of Your Next Trade Show Investment," would be of interest to someone who has dropped a bunch of money to exhibit at a trade show and is now stressing about the ROI. Put a gated lead-generation landing page in front of the access to the white paper and you'll collect contact info on some great prospects for your digital/inkjet print solutions. You could also go "negative" and make the title, "Five Mistakes Exhibitors Make at a Trade Show." Why does it matter? Because we live in a busy world and decisions will be made based solely on the title. Make it interesting and provocative.

2. *Blog*

    We'll mention a blog as a possibility, however it does not lend itself to being a great medium for marketing your digital/inkjet printing capabilities. That is, there are better options. Blogs are stream-of-consciousness brand-builders. Write a blog if you have something of interest to say. Keep it to around 250 words and, again, consider the fact that it will be judged—and read— on the basis of the title you give it.

3. *Case Studies*

    The best way to portray this option is as the script to one of your YouTube videos: "Here's a problem we solved for someone else. Cool, huh? Call us." Printed case studies are also effective.

4. *Printed Newsletters*

    Yes, there is still room for the old-fashioned newsletter, especially if it demonstrates the value of digital/inkjet printing. That is, what can you do with this opportunity to show off? Personalize it using your digital/inkjet press? Imprint on an offset-printed shell and demonstrate versioning?

Content creation is a hungry monster that constantly needs feeding. What's more, it matters that your communication is clear and correct. A typo can kill your attempt to demonstrate advanced skills. Double and triple check for errors. Steve Martin said it best: "Some people have a way with words. Others not have way."

Moving on...

An Open House

You probably cleaned up your shop to put the pretty new machine in, so now is a great time to show off. This does not have to be the kind of thing event that costs a lot of money. You can have it catered or run to Costco (more on that in a second). You will invite everyone on your client list and your prospects. You will carefully consider the calendar and avoid school vacations, major sports events, and holidays. Your team will sport matching polos with your company logo on them. Everyone will be trained on how to talk to customers, and you will display many great examples of projects you have completed. You will give tours, and you might even hire a speaker or two. You absolutely should involve your paper vendors, the people you bought the machine from and any other suppliers you give lots of money to on a regular basis. They should jump at the chance to help you be more successful (and might even pitch in for the cost). Be specific about what you want them to do. Do you want them to help with demos? Give a quick talk about substrates? Present some great case studies? The machines will be humming. Plan a schedule of activities, and make sure that guests who have never been to your shop will be impressed and entertained. You'll never be prouder of your staff, your building and your company. Have fun with it!

An Educational Event or Series

Are there recurring problems that you typically see in files that come from clients? Are there client issues popping up again and again about color management, paper choices, or mailing lists? If so, these should be red flags that scream *opportunity* to you. Instead of getting mad, get "teachy" – Invite creatives and creators to come at lunch time, order some food, and teach them what they need to know. Ask them to bring a friend, maybe someone at another agency, a colleague, or anyone else they think might benefit from learning. Strange tip: If you are going to do this regularly, invest some money on the food, the best you can afford, even going so far as to hire a good caterer. As crazy as it sounds, you want to make this a must-attend event. Good food attracts, as one Northern Plains printer learned (to the point where they actually charged for it!).

Outside Speaking Engagements

This is where things get fun. While potentially terrifying, take it from two veteran presenters: You want to get in front of people and talk like a subject matter expert. Each gig leads to a new opportunity. You might not be a very polished speaker at first. We certainly weren't. But, eventually, you will learn to connect knowledge with an audience. Here are some examples of audiences that you probably have but have just never thought of before:

1. A networking group that you belong to or have been meaning to join
2. A trade association (of yours—for the practice— OR even better, that of your clients)
3. A chamber of commerce or local business group
4. Any volunteer or civic organizations that you belong to or have worked with in the past
5. An adult education program in your town or a neighboring city

Now here are a few stipulations about these speaking opportunities. They are NOT sales presentations where you speak directly about your products and services. There is no "I-me-my" in these talks. You do not talk about your equipment. These talks are meant to educate about a broader topic, application, or technology that a group of people want to learn more about.

Here would be some examples of titles to a talk you might be qualified to give:

1. 5 Ways to Use New Printing Technologies to Grow and Promote Your Business
2. Debunking Myths About Print and Sustainability
3. Print's Not Dead!
4. New Customers Now – How Direct Mail Will Get Your Phone Ringing

You get the picture. Speaking in front of a group is empowering; it brings you closer to your community, customers and prospects; and it makes you a better salesperson. Make it a goal to do so whenever, and as much, as you can.

A Sales Plan

Chances are, some readers of this book may have skipped the introduction, briefly reviewed the fundamentals, done a "yeah-yeah, whatever" through the section on marketing, and jumped right to this sales plan. That's fine. We're salespeople, too, and understand the kinship shared with this particular subject. We'd probably do the same thing if we were you. Everyone wants to know how to sell digital/inkjet output. But before we get to the meat, we need to cover something discussed earlier. Namely, the fact that salespeople really don't want to sell digital/inkjet. We've already talked about why that is, now let's discuss what to do about it.

First, get the reps comfortable with digital/inkjet technology. They won't sell what they don't understand, so start with a basic level of knowledge/comfort, talk applications, and end with the nuances that exist within specific vertical markets.

The best way for them to get comfortable is to understand the applications. And we're not just talking about a passing knowledge of applications. We are talking about knowing them cold. In and out. Forwards and backwards. Up and down. Inside and...You get the point. Tell stories. Everyone loves a good story.

A good way to start is to give some real-life examples how a digital/inkjet printing solution solved a problem or met a business need. By learning the before and after, and discussing the difference digital/inkjet printing made, salespeople will not only understand where it fits, they'll have a starting point for seeking new orders. Given the fact that digital printing has been around now for a couple of decades, it shouldn't be hard to find some success stories. If you get stuck, your digital/inkjet press vendor should be able to help.

To further drill the point home that selling digital/inkjet printing profitably is about solving problems, your next step should be to discuss one of the key concepts we covered earlier: the 20/1 ratio. To review, this concept compares the price of purchasing a given printed piece ($1) and the cost of using that piece from start to finish ($20). Talk to your salespeople about the kinds of costs that might make up that $20 area (waste, obsolescence, etc.) so they understand how to talk to clients about it and can later justify the higher per piece cost of digital/inkjet versus traditional offset. In addition to understanding the concept that digital/inkjet and VDP have a growing place in the print world, they should know some basic facts and data about the press itself. An immersion program of paper stocks, speeds and feeds, and finishing capabilities of your specific machine is a great idea. It's kind of a "the more you know" kind of thing. The vendors (equipment and paper) have likely given this speech before and can be of tremendous assistance here.

The truth is, though, that selling digital/inkjet output is not that much different than selling conventional printing. At its core, your customers have a need, and your shop will meet that need with a digital/inkjet solution. Your reps need to remember that. If anything, they should be celebrating the fact that the digital/inkjet equipment has opened a whole lot of new opportunities for them to capture projects that, up until now, were not in your wheelhouse.

But all the knowledge and understanding in the world won't make any difference if the sales rep has a fundamental belief that it's not worth his or her time. To change that, it's time to play the ace card.

Sales Compensation

Don't overthink this, gang. Salespeople follow the money. Period. If you have a sales background, you get this. However, if you come from the world of Accounting or Engineering, this very well might be the first time you are hearing this news. But you can take it to the sales bank. Trust us on this: The only way you're going to get your salespeople to be at all interested is if you make it worth their time financially. They don't care that the equipment is expensive. They don't care that your company took a risk. They care about what's in it for them. Sorry (not sorry), but the same things that make a sales rep successful can also manifest itself as selfish, dominant, calculating, and other unattractive characteristics. You don't need to like your reps. You need them to be good at what they do. If you like them, that's a bonus.

A commercial printer in New England installed a digital/inkjet press some years ago and Bill was engaged to help make it successful. At the time, there were 12 full-time salespeople. Quickly realizing the sales team did not share in Management's enthusiasm for this new venture, they devised a clever sales compensation plan designed to get and keep the sales reps' attention:

$100 Cash Bonus
For the first digital order entered, regardless of size

$500 Cash Bonus
When same customer's digital sales hit $3,500

$500 Cash Bonus
When same customer's digital sales hit $7,000

$5,000 Cash Bonus
When same customer's digital sales hit $100,000

To grease the skids, each salesperson was given two $500 coupons for free digital work. This approach encouraged the reps to discuss digital/inkjet with existing clients—the shallow end of the risk pool. By using this special comp plan, the company did everything it could to motivate the sales force financially.

The concept of money-based motivation is an important lesson for Management to understand, especially if said Management does not come from a sales background. Your first step, then, and best sales tip for engaging the sales force, is to overcompensate using commissions as a motivator.

One thing you might want to try, in addition to the aforementioned incentive plan, is to give each rep SOME sort of metric to hit with regard to digital/inkjet. Whether it's a number of new opportunities, a number of new clients, or a dollar figure, collaboratively get them to agree to put some skin in the game. You also know that salespeople tend to be competitive with one another, so make a game out of it.

Kelly sat in on a sales meeting where a sales manager gave out a $100 Visa gift card to the rep who won some contest earlier in the month, and I swear you would have thought the manager was passing out Apple Watches for how excited they all got for the sales rep who won. Salespeople LOVE to win and they love free stuff.

Bill's Side Story:

> I have been a regular seminar speaker at Graph Expo/Print for 20 years. One year, just as I was about to begin my presentation, a couple walked in and headed directly for the front row, straight up the center aisle. The man found a seat while the woman walked up to me and said something to the effect of, "I came and heard you talk about digital/inkjet printing last year. You held your wallet in the air and said, 'If you want to get your salespeople to sell digi-

tal/inkjet, use this as your microphone.' I came back this year and dragged my husband along so that he could hear it for himself. We were unsuccessful at motivating our salespeople a year ago and nothing has changed." Despite the fact that my seminar title was, "The 25 Best Print Sales Tips Ever" and was not supposed to have anything to do with selling digital/inkjet, I still managed to work it in. The last thing I wanted was that woman all up in my face on the way out the door the way she was on the way coming in.

Now that the sales reps are properly incentivized, let's point them in the right direction and help find the best sources for leads.

Know where to look
There are two ways to look at the subject of where to look for digital/inkjet printing prospects. First, we can provide a list of vertical industries that are most likely to purchase digital/inkjet printing. It would only be logical, then, that we next name the kinds of specific applications typically bought. But there's a problem with that thinking: It leads to the price objection. We'll explain...

Suppose you knew that banks bought digital/inkjet output. How do you know? Bill and Kelly told you. So, you pick up the phone, call Purchasing, and set up an appointment to make an in-person visit (in this fantasy world, the Buyer picked up on the first ring and she had plenty of time for you). In that meeting, you ask about their digital/inkjet printing needs and are given the chance to provide pricing. You subsequently make a quick trip back to the shop armed with the specs of the job, and the price is generated and emailed to the client. She responds right away with the bad news: Your price is too high.

What happened? What went wrong? Plenty! First you are guilty of "selling printing." That is, you are attempting to win business based on a low price. Instead, you should be focused on solving problems by understanding their business needs. Second, your approach was completely backwards. You put the "Who?"—Who buys the printing?—before the "What?"—What are their business needs?—and sought out the buyer of the piece instead of its originator.

The correct approach for identifying sources and leads for selling digital/inkjet printing is to first sharpen your selling skills to where you are taking a 100% consultative approach. This selling method is solutions-based and can be achieved only when you understand what their business is about, what they are trying to do, what their priorities are, and what they are doing to increase revenues (a.k.a., the "What?"). We will once again direct you towards Bill's book, "The 25 Best Print Sales Tips Ever!" to help you with this endeavor and get back to the question of where to look for the best leads.

The ideal customer for your digital/inkjet printing solutions is technically competent, creative, has an accurate database (if you are selling VDP, that is), and sees you as a solutions provider. When you discussed the 20/1 ratio with this prospect, the buyer grasped the concept. They get it.

Also important is to understand the features and benefits of digital/inkjet so that you can better find companies that can truly benefit. For example, one feature is economical production of high-quality print in low quantities. The accompanying benefit is that it could allow a marketing department or a product manager to test several different messages at once, before shifting to a longer-run campaign. With that information in hand, the next step would be to find companies with that need.

Quick turnaround. Consistent quality. Low cost at low quantity. This is what clients get when they opt for your digital/inkjet printing solutions. That is your cure, your vitamin E. What you need next is to find the disease. Let's talk about the best places to look.

This first source requires a mea culpa from Bill...

> "When we first started teaming up many years ago to create a digital printing training curriculum, I asked Kelly to come up with some sources for prospects. At the top of her list was one that made me groan: Your Library. When I saw it I thought to myself, 'Does she not understand we are in a digital age?' But after hearing Kelly explain her thinking I realized Ms. Mallozzi was a genius of some kind. Over the years, we have given this advice in many forms and to many people and, without question, it is the Number One most helpful tip for finding great leads for selling digital/inkjet printing. There. Is that enough groveling, Kelly?" *Kelly's reply: "No, Bill, but it's a start."*

1. Your Library

The Library is an untapped resource of gold of which no one is using for what you want. Walk into your local public library and march over to the reference librarian. Before you sits an individual who went to college to learn how to find information. Describe the kinds of companies you are looking for (especially after you read the section about selling to vertical markets) and provide as much detail as possible. Tell your new BFF that you'll be back in a few days. When you return, we guarantee you will be surprised at what you'll be handed. Waiting for you will be a list of companies or organizations in the geographic area you designated— all of which will be ripe for the picking. (Then, don't forget to send an email to Kelly and remind her of her genius.)

2. Google
The discussion of where to look for prospects really does not have to extend much further than Google. You will again need to know the value of digital/inkjet output and how it relates to the kinds of markets you desire.

We are going to try to talk you through this as if we were sitting down next to one another at a computer. Let's say you decided that retailers were a vertical market that you wanted to pursue this year, and that your most successful area of the country is the Northeast. We just googled "top retailers in the Northeast" and were brought to a page called The Shelby Report www.theshelbyreport.com/2012/09/13/consultant-describes-what-a-top-grocery-retailer-looks-like/top-25-ne/

We now have a list of the largest grocery chains, along with the number of stores they have and their weekly sales. We can continue with these 25 companies as prospects. However, if we want to investigate other types of retailers, we google "top non-grocery retailers in the Northeast" and find ourselves at the National Retail Federation webpage. https://nrf.com/news/stores-magazine. Simple!

3. LinkedIn
LinkedIn is the single greatest repository of who's who in the business world. And it's free. Here is just a smattering of what you can discover in minutes:
- Where someone works
- How long that person has been there
- Promotions he/she has had
- Where the individual went to school

- What volunteer work he/she does or has done
- Who his/her co-workers are
- Other people who have held the same job
- Other companies in the same business
- Other key people who work there

See? It is a veritable rabbit hole of valuable information. But only use LinkedIn after you have researched the company, considered its business needs, and already defined the "Who?" It's a rabbit hole because you can fall down it and feel like you will never find your way out, but in a good way. If you dedicate time, every single day, to using LinkedIn, not only will you get really good at navigating it quickly, you will just naturally build your own network while at the same time always come away with new leads, new ideas, and new connections. Winning!

Know What to Say in Order to Gain Appointments
Okay, now you've got a pocket full of prospects. You know the names of companies and organizations that you believe would benefit from the value of a digital/inkjet printing solution. Your next step involves the single most important selling skill any print sales rep can have, regardless of whether they sell digital/inkjet or traditional offset—that of pre-call research. It's your knowledge of the company's needs, goals, and direction that will first get you in the door and later help generate profitable and repeatable digital/inkjet printing sales. Only by first understanding what it is they are trying to do can you aim your sales pitch in the proper direction. Here's a simple example to help prove the point...

Bill and Kelly have written a best-selling book, *Who's Making Money at Digital/Inkjet Printing... and How?* and are now rich and famous. You want to call on them. That last paragraph told you that you first need to figure out what they are trying to do (Dale Carnegie thinking: You can get what you want when you figure out what the other guy wants and help him to get it.) That's not difficult. After writing their books, authors want to find ways to sell them. Putting all of these thoughts together, you come up with this sales pitch: "The purpose of my call is to talk to you about how I can help you sell your new book using the capabilities of our digital/inkjet printing equipment." Without having first considered the business need(s) of the prospect, your sales call is reduced to calling on buyers and quoting specifications (a.k.a. "selling print"). Learning what to say in order to gain appointments demands a selling skill that most print salespeople don't have.

It's also imperative to know how to gather information on a company by viewing their website and learning about their specific industry prior to the start of any prospecting process. A company's website is a window to their soul. It is their main communication tool and contains all of the information you will need to form the best possible sales call. There, you will learn about a company's business needs and growth strategies, product announcements and upcoming events. By reading various announcements and press releases—and even reading between the lines—you'll get a basic understanding and find the best way to finish the sentence that starts, "The purpose of my call is...," with a strong, appointment-getting statement. Acquiring this skill not only allows the salesperson to sell digital/inkjet printing profitably, but also all of his or her products and services profitably.

How to Create a Prospecting Process
Of the nearly 500 people who have taken the sales assessment test that sits at AspireFor.com, 90% confessed that they have no prospecting process whatsoever. Ninety percent! Instead, they make random and occasional sales calls if they have free time and during the down times when they need to drum up some new business. How's that for a strategy?

The good news is two-fold. First, there is no such thing as a digital/inkjet printing prospecting process. That is, what works for selling print in general will also work for selling digital/inkjet print. Second, there is no one-size-fits-all, guaranteed-to-work, step-by-step, week-by-week prospecting process. This means you can put together a series of sales activities and, as long as you apply them with diligence and pleasant persistence, you'll find success. You will also need a first step, follow-up activities, and a stopping point. We recommend an anecdotal approach, one that tells a success story and promises follow-up. Then, by phone, email, and even stopping by in-person, keep driving home the message that you've got something of value to say. At some point, and that point is typically after four to six weeks, stop and reassess. Should you continue? Should you stop altogether? That's your call, but we'll give you this measuring stick: How badly do you want to do business with them? If only a little, then prospect only a little. If a lot, maybe take a little break and check in periodically.

Effective Sales Presentation Skills for Digital/Inkjet
You have finally earned an appointment with a high potential, digital/inkjet printing prospect. Congratulations! Now what?

The digital/inkjet printing appointment—the one where you are making a presentation—is the same in terms of approach, content and delivery, with one key exception. Now, you need to prove this to be the better print solution. If you've done your homework and truly understand the story behind the printed pieces they require, you stand a much better chance of making the sale for the simple reason that you can apply the benefits of digital/inkjet and demonstrate how it helps the customer to better meet their needs.

Similar to the marketing of digital/inkjet printing, presenting its value in a sales call requires the art of good storytelling. You need to paint the picture, playing up the benefits. Why? Because the client is almost certainly giving something up and you want to make certain what they're gaining in return more than makes up for any loss. Plus—and this is no small point—there is a huge fear factor when it comes to switching to digital/inkjet output. An effective sales presentation keeps this in mind, especially as it sets up our next point—objections.

How to Overcome Objections

Wikipedia defines the word "objection" as "a request for more information." Keep this in mind when you consider a response to the following possible statements you'll likely hear from prospects and customers.

1. "I don't understand digital/inkjet technology."
It's highly unlikely you'll hear someone use this exact statement. Rarely will you find someone brave enough to utter the words. Instead, you might hear something irrational or nonsensical doubting the validity of your arguments, but what it comes down to is: they don't have a clear picture of what digital/inkjet printing is and what it can do for them. If you know someone to be on the lower end of the technically-savvy measuring stick (a flip phone sitting on their desk would be a dead giveaway), simply assume that this is the case and include a recap of the basics of digital/inkjet printing in your response. You want to illustrate examples of companies, very similar to theirs, which have successfully implemented digital/inkjet print procurement. Also make sure to give them a happy ending in which the company's goals were realized and fears were smashed to bits.

2. "I don't believe digital/inkjet output is as good as conventional."
By "good" we assume the customer means quality. Digital/inkjet printing has come an awfully long way in closing the gap

between it and traditional offset. That reality, however, might not be enough to overcome this objection. The right approach to this objection is proving digital/inkjet to be acceptable for this particular application. Perhaps you want to give them your best version of the Pepsi challenge, in which you show the client or prospect the same piece of artwork printed on several different presses and ask the individual to rank them in order of quality with the naked eye. NO loupes allowed. This will take some work on your part and the entire sales team should be armed with these sample kits. Your equipment vendors should be able to help you get sets of these samples printed by different processes from their showrooms and training floors. Digital/Inkjet equipment vendors are likely sources for good print samples.

3. *"I am old, lazy and thus don't want to learn anything new."* This objection is more likely to sound like, "We've always done it this way and have never had a problem. So, I see no reason to switch." Such a stance is all about fear and not wanting to expand their horizons or take any risks. Remove the fear and you'll remove the obstacle. Again, an anecdotal approach should work wonders here. If you have another client who was similarly skeptical and fearful, relate that story. Make the customer understand that you will be there every step of the way, with proofs and press samples, and make it personal. Promise that things will be okay, and guarantee they'll be happy or they can go back to the old way of doing things no worse for wear. Also use facts. There are some great statistics and facts and figures available about the widespread growth and continued rise of digital/inkjet printing, so use that in your messaging. Clients and prospects don't want to be left in the dust if all the cool kids (and even old folks) are now on the digital train. You might even make it personal, describing the evolution of smart phones or Amazon as examples of ubiquitous progress. If all else fails, be direct: "What is it you're afraid of when it comes

to a digital/inkjet option?" Sometimes going right down Main Street is the best approach.

4. "Digital/inkjet is more expensive."
The most important phrase you can use to illustrate the power of digital/inkjet printing is, "It's not what it costs, it's what it's worth." If you are dealing with a person who has spent his/her entire 30-year career buying printing by choosing the lowest cost per thousand, all is not lost. Remember, we also advocate a discussion at a higher level with different people in the buyer's organization—individuals who better understand that a given printed piece has a mission, and you are here to help that piece realize its full potential. So just say that. Even a print buyer who buys on the cheap can be helped to understand the reality of spending more per thousand to accomplish things like waste reduction, higher efficiencies, and saving the planet. Use personal examples to help illustrate the point. Most people are willing to spend more on certain things if what they are getting as a result means something. Luxury cars and clothes, organic food, and real estate are good examples of this. So, if you can, dig a little deeper in to the buyer's personal life in order to draw a parallel to something he/she does personally to help illustrate that it makes sense to do that with digital/inkjet as well. Move away from cost conversation as fast as possible and get back to what got you here, the problem being solved better by a digital/inkjet solution.

Section Two: Summary
If your takeaway from this section is something akin to, "A lot of this is just common sense," you're definitely catching on. What it takes is mostly a realignment back to the business of helping your customers find their customers using the best means and smartest solutions possible. Digital/inkjet printing technology is simply another tool in the toolbox. That's it. So, now that you know the formula, let's compare where you want to be with where you are.

SECTION THREE

Your Action Plan

Section Three: Your Action Plan

Hopefully by now, the book you are holding in your hand has been dog-eared and is full of notes in the margins. Words are underlined, entire paragraphs are circled, words like "Brilliant!" and "Great idea!" and "Gosh, these authors are frigging savants. Who will play them in the movie?" are sprinkled among the pages. In general, your head is spinning from all of the information that is sure to make you the success story we will write about in the book's sequel. So that you leave with a plan, we offer this section to help with your organization. And then, to help you to find profitability fast, we've included an Addendum detailing five vertical markets and how to sell digital/inkjet printing using the techniques included in the last section. But first, the plan...

Much of your success in this or any endeavor has to do with preparation. Too often, a digital/inkjet piece of equipment is installed before all the factors have been taken into consideration. This was very much the case in the early days of digital printing. Press manufacturers offered free trials and a few months of no click charge in an effort to get their equipment on the floor before the competition could. Without a chip in the game, however, printers had no incentive to seek success and the box collected dust. And without the skills necessary to find profitability, they sold orders based on price—and the race to the bottom was on. Today, printers enter the digital/inkjet world with their eyes wide open, considering all aspects of the endeavor and with the benefit of not being the first to walk across the frozen lake, only to find the ice isn't thick enough to support them.

We wrote this book for two primary audiences: owners/presidents and salespeople. As such, this section will include self-assessment advice for both. Some of it is exactly the same and some is unique to that group. Pick one. While you read, listen to that little voice in your head (or perhaps that feeling in the pit of your stomach). What is it telling you? Don't ignore even the slightest sense that a box is unchecked. You don't stick your toe in digital waters. You dive in and either swim or drown. No pressure, though.

One last thing. Once upon a time, the expectations for turnaround was weeks. Time was a lot slower. Today, when someone is asked, "When do you want it?" a calendar is no longer consulted to assist in the answer. Now it's a watch. All of this is to say, speed plays a part in every aspect of the new digital world. Can you handle an order from quote to prepress to print to finishing in days? Great! But what happens when your digital business takes off? The first time your crank out a job in 48 hours, you'll be a hero. But that sets the bar awfully high. Can you sustain that level of service? Just something to keep in mind as you ponder.

For Owners/Presidents

Step One: Consider your technical superiority to your competition

A wise man once said, "You do the free things first, the cheap things second, and then you spend the money." Free, in this case, involves thoughtful consideration of your company's assets, customer base, competitive landscape, and overall digital future. Cheap might be an investment of time sitting with vendors, attending a trade show or association meeting, perhaps even trying out the equipment. Following this pattern, by the time you spend the money, your chances of success skyrocket.
Let's get you ready:

If you are the owner or company president, you have your own viewpoint on this first subject, but there are three other opinions that also matter: Your salespeople, customers, and employees. Each has their own perspective and you should seek honest appraisal in order to form a well-rounded assessment. This being a critical aspect to digital print success, we suggest you spend considerable time on this point.

There are three things to consider: The equipment, the staff, and the workflow. Ideally, you have all of the best and latest fire-power—computers and software—to handle what the client will throw at you and a prepress staff that has the right combination of skill, training, and attitude. Ideally. And then, there is reality. So, let's assess...

Questions to ask:

1. Do we have the right equipment?
2. Do we have enough equipment to handle our workload?
3. Do we have a contingency plan to handle a possible over-load?
4. Do we have expertise in the right software?
5. What is the competency level of the employees in the pre-press department?
6. What ongoing training currently takes place?
7. Is there a knowledge deficiency?
8. Is there a consistent workflow bottleneck in prepress?
9. Is there a capability that our competition has that we don't
10. Do we cross-train so that we have a backup in the event of a temporary or permanent loss of a key employee?
11. The most important question to ask yourself, your sales reps, and your customers is this: Is our prepress depart-ment a strength or liability to our company?

Step Two: Consider your staff

This next aspect to think about is personnel. Do you have the right people in the right places? Starting with the sales team and continuing right through customer service, estimators, press operators, bindery, and shipping, consider your staff and pay special attention to the fact that the customer expectation is rapid turnarounds and instant information access, not exactly the print industry's hallmark. Is everyone up to the task?

Questions to ask:

1. What is the attitude of each salesperson regarding digital/inkjet printing? Note: they are likely to share different opinions publicly versus privately. Seek both.

2. How would I rate their willingness to learn and sell digital/inkjet output first to their existing accounts rather than go after new business?

3. Will I need an entirely different sales force?

4. Can profitability be found without any direct sales force at all, only via marketing efforts?

5. Can my Estimator keep up with an increased work-load and shorter turnaround times for pricing?

6. Are my CSRs up to the task? Are they ready for the pace of digital?

7. Do we have an existing team member who can run a digital/inkjet press or will I need someone new?

8. Do we have someone who can handle our marketing, especially the ability to develop a social media presence?

9. Do we have someone who can create content (blogs, White Papers, Testimonials)?

Step Three: Consider your marketing efforts
The Achilles' heel of the printing industry is marketing our own services. We are notoriously bad at practicing what we preach. Your company likely suffers in this category, just like everyone else. Crafting the right message (and believe us, "We've got digital!" ain't it!) is critical to your success. This is likely to be an entirely new endeavor for you since you have probably talked

the talk, but not walked the walk, when it comes to marketing. We urge you to invest sufficient time and money in this area. Do your homework. Do the free things first: Find out what others are doing either through a Google search, by tapping into your PIA affiliate network, or by joining a LinkedIn group and posting a question. This is yet another area where you can benefit from not being on the bleeding edge.

Questions to ask:

1. What marketing, if any, are we doing currently?

2. What has the result been?

3. What is the status of our database of prospects and existing clients?

4. How accurate is it?

5. What is our presence on social media?

6. What success stories could we tell?

7. Do we have any testimonials?

Step Four: Consider your company

This might seem like an esoteric exercise but take a look at your company as a whole. Prior to the time that you put your first digital piece of equipment on the floor, who were you? If you had a defined purpose—a brand—what was it? What was/is your differentiator? Adding digital/inkjet printing capabilities changes everything. This can either augment what you've got going or can serve as a reset button, allowing you to head off in a different direction. You can still be customer-focused. You can still be all about solutions. But a new capability—one that shortens turnaround times—adds an urgency to the mix and can create a fundamental change within the core of your company.

The most notable and impactful difference comes in your brand. You have one, whether intentional or not. You have a reputation. In fact, there are likely several viewpoints on what you are as a company. So that you can truly understand both the impact and the potential for change, poll your customer base (or hire an outside service to ask for you). In the end, their opinion is the only thing that matters.

We pointed out earlier that digital/inkjet printing is like vitamin E, a cure looking for a disease. Adding digital capabilities will give you options never before possible, potentially unlocking creative doors. It'd be like living in a house for years and then learning there is an entirely different section you never knew existed until one day a wall came down.

Questions to ask customers:

1. Why do you currently do business with us?

2. What do you feel is our differentiator?

3. What is our greatest strength? Weakness?

4. What would you want us to do that we aren't?

Step Five: Consider your sales plan
It's no accident that we list this bullet point last. All of the digital/inkjet printing firepower in the world means nothing if your sales team lacks the ability to sell its benefits.

As Bill points out in his first book, *The 25 Best Print Sales Tips Ever!*, there are four keys to sales success:

1. A high-value, well-researched sales call

2. The right target market

3. A prospecting process

4. Diligence and pleasant persistence

An effective sales plan, the thing that's going to make all of this effort worth it, requires a solutions-based approach. "Do you have any digital/inkjet print jobs we could quote on?" is akin to relying on low price to win orders. The digital equipment vendor earns a click charge either way. They win, at least in the short-term, if you use this strategy. The customer wins if you use this pricing strategy. Only you, the digital print provider, loses.

Since the best indicator of the future is to look into the past, it's important that you examine your existing sales plan. How does your company stand on those four sales keys? Rate yourself on a scale of 1 to 10. Ask others on your management team to do the same. Then, focus on the lowest numbers.

We simply cannot stress enough the need to apply the spotlight to your sales plan prior to the installation of any digital/inkjet printing equipment. If you've gotten anything at all from this book, you know to measure the distance between where you are from a technical and sales standpoint to where you need to be and not underestimate the importance of eliminating the gap. This is not just another piece or iron. This is a game-changer.

There are two ways to look at your final assessment. The result can be a problem or it can be an opportunity. This could be a minor adjustment, or a chance for you to make a major overhaul. If you don't like what you see as you peel back the onion, consider throwing the whole thing away and starting over. That is, use your decision to buy your first or subsequent digital/inkjet equipment as a course correction, completely rebranding in recommitting yourself, your staff, and your profits to a new and better future.

Now, let's look at the assessment process and advice salespeople should undertake...

Sales Reps & Selling Owners

As a salesperson, you have frontline responsibility for making this move to digital/inkjet a success. Countless hours and a boatload of money have been spent selecting, purchasing, and installing the equipment. Failure on your part to profitably sell the output could result in disaster.

To review the "Why should you care?" issue, remember that your work (selling digital/inkjet) is all upfront. Once a client is turned on to digital and connected to your company, orders come in often without your knowledge. You have built an annuity, one that pays dividends in the form of ongoing commissions.

While this is oversimplification of the selling process, the three most important aspects are:

1. Where to look for leads

2. What to say in order to gain an appointment

3. An effective prospecting process

We've given the company president and upper management their marching orders for making this endeavor a success; now let's go over your salesperson checklist:

Step One: Consider your attitude

Assuming you read this book voluntarily, you are probably already on board with the idea of accepting the challenge of selling digital/inkjet printing. As such, the real assessment should be in other areas. But if you are reading these pages while at the end of a bayonet and you have already made up your mind that you will hate the technology, own it. That's an important admission. We could take a Tom Sawyer approach and tell you, "Not everyone can do it properly. It takes a special kind of salesperson" and hope that being passive aggressive motivates you. But if you've made it through our first 20,412 words and you are still not on board, there might be nothing more we can do. So, while others are making money in creating steady revenue streams, how about you go sit in the corner and wonder why the screen on your PalmPilot isn't as fast as it used to be.

Within the confines of this book, no one is judging you. Were this a live presentation, we might ask you to publicly state your viewpoint. But since that is not the case, you are free to be completely honest with yourself and hold your answers private if you so choose. But know this: If you don't bring digital solutions to your clients, someone else will and they probably have offset capabilities as well. Is your resistance to digital such that you are ready to lose entire clients?

A commercial print sales force of 10 is likely to have only one or two reps who are eagerly and actively engaged in the process of digital/inkjet printing sales. If you are in that one or two "I love digital!" group, great. If not, seek them out and learn everything you can. Among the eight or nine who choose not to participate, there are some who lack the skill, others who lack the will, and some who lack both. Consider again the question we posed to management. We asked about the attitude of each sales rep regarding digital/inkjet printing. If your mind is completely shut, whether it's out of fear of being exposed as a flip phone-using technological Neanderthal, or you just don't see the need to pursue new opportunities that don't come from your existing customer base, we hope you are in your mid-60s and have a healthy 401(k). If not, the longer you wait, the scarier this becomes. The key is to admit your hesitation and embrace the opportunity to look down a new and profitable path. Do the free things first.

Step Two: Consider your ability to identify digital printing applications (where to look for leads).
You've got existing, and perhaps new, digital/inkjet presses on the floor. Congratulations. Who cares? We're not being flippant here; we are asking a real question: Who is going to care about the ben-

efits of digital/inkjet printing capabilities? You are going to need some suitable targets and, regardless of whether they come from the equipment vendor, your marketing department or through your own investigatory efforts, it's important that you understand who buys this stuff and why.

Stop there for a second. That last sentence had carefully chosen words: "... who buys this stuff and why." This is different than just understanding the applications. In the Addendum that follows this assessment, we will discuss specific vertical markets and reveal how to sell digital/inkjet printing to each. For now, ponder your ability to identify the need for digital, both within your existing customers and any new opportunities. What kind of help will you need? Can you spot a digital/inkjet application? Are you able to hold a basic conversation? At a bare minimum, we want you to be digital dogs, sniffing out and pointing to opportunities (standard dog-pointing positioning is optional) and then step aside to let your technical people do their techie thing.

Step Three: Consider your current "sales entry point" (what to say in order to gain an appointment).
Now, there's a term that you probably haven't heard before (mostly because we just made it up on the spot). The sales entry point has to do with where along the food chain you currently live with your existing accounts. Do you seek out the traditional Print Buyer and try to provide pricing? Is the Buyer your key contact? If so, you live at the quote stage of the job. Or perhaps you seek out a Decision-Maker and present a new idea based on the pre-call research you have done? Sure, you know and work with the Buyer, but you are deeply connected within a company. If this description is more you, you live at the design stage.

Like we told the Owners/Presidents in their assessment section, the best indicator of the future is to take a close look at the past. It's doubtful that you will suddenly sprout superior sales skills (say that three times fast!). For now, be aware of your existing approach and think about how you would attack a new account. Digital/Inkjet solutions are seldom cheaper since the quantity is typically less than traditional offset. This means you've got some 'splainin' to do, Lucy, and that means solving and not selling.

The single most important skill a sales rep can have is the ability to research a company prior to the start of the prospecting process and gain an understanding of their business needs. Then, using that knowledge, the solutions-based sales rep makes a sales call based on an idea to either lower the usage cost of the document or increase its value.

The point is, new iron isn't automatically going to change your sales approach in the same way new golf clubs don't instantly improve your swing. If you currently sell on price, this is how you will sell digital/inkjet. If you are more solutions-focused, that habit is also likely to continue. But let's not lose all hope. Keep your head down, left elbow straight, and put some effort into becoming a better salesperson. And remember to follow through.

Step Four: Consider your current prospecting process
Do you even have one? Ninety percent of you don't. If you count yourself in that massive majority, make a change. When selling digital/inkjet printing to new customers, what will you do first? Then, what will you do next? And what about after that?

Here's the good news: The steps themselves (email, phone call, text, etc.) are less important than the frequency with which they are applied. This means you can put together any combo platter of selling activities and so long as you are diligent about their application, you will find success. Remember, this is an anecdotal sale. Starting your process with a success story is a good way to get into the right conversations. Just a thought...

Step Five: Consider your personal marketing plan
Our conversation regarding marketing digital/inkjet printing

included the concept that you, too, should be building a brand and stocking the pond. Is this skill in your wheelhouse? Now, in the event you saw the word "marketing" and skipped ahead out of fear that you'd fall asleep while reading, a quick reminder: What we are talking about here, at bare minimum, might be the creation of a quick YouTube video featuring a success story. This could be a few slides with a voiceover. Upload a PowerPoint presentation and voilà, you can send someone a link as a part of your prospecting process. A phone call might not get through and a voicemail won't be returned, but a two-minute video embedded into an email might just do the trick. Other options could be writing white papers or success stories that put the benefits of digital/inkjet printing in the right light. Do you have any mad skills in this area?

Step Six: Consider your technical skill set
As stated, there are lots of reasons why people will buy from you. At or near the top will be your company's reputation and ability from a technical standpoint. That is, are you able to handle all types of print files? We've put others in charge of studying the existing mix of equipment, staff, and expertise. That leaves you to look in the mirror and ask, what does the person I'm looking at need in terms of technical skills to sell digital/inkjet printing?

Let us be clear. It is by no means necessary that you have the ability to manipulate complicated files. In fact, no one wants you that deeply involved. Yours needs to be a far more superficial understanding of electronic print files. It's like being conversational in French. Perhaps you want to learn enough to order a glass of rosé, but you don't need to be able to get into an argument with a snooty maître d' over why their menu has neither toast nor fries, and they still call themselves a French restaurant.

Ideally, you are able to answer some simple questions from the customer, such as which software programs you take and how best to deliver the files. The lack of knowledge in this area erodes client confidence since you are the face of the company. The solution to a lack of skills in this area is a simple fix, so for now be honest with yourself in your self-assessment. The last thing you want to do is overstate your abilities because your ego won't let you admit a weakness, only to find a digital/inkjet print sale evaporates because you don't have the answer to a simple question about a file.

SECTION FOUR

Final Thoughts

Section Four: Final Thoughts

This book was written by two people with one voice ("we think" and "we suggest"). We tried, up until now, to stay away from sharing individual opinions or thoughts. To wrap things up and stick the landing, we thought it would be appropriate to abandon that approach and offer up a few final messages before getting to the vertical markets. Ladies first...

From the desk of Kelly Mallozzi:

Subject: So, what does this mean?

As with the advent of digital printing some 30 years ago, we are in the midst of a massive paradigm shift when it comes to how any person today interacts with customers and prospects. These shifts are never easy nor are they simple, nor do the results happen overnight. What this means for you is that you might have to completely overhaul what you are saying, how you are saying it, and who you are saying it to. Yes. This is revolutionary. It will require you to break some habits. It might require you to get some help, either from a colleague, a mentor, or maybe even from strangers on the internet. This book is a great starting point, but it is just that. A starting point. Pretty soon, hopefully even tomorrow, it will be time for you to chart a new course and start sharpening a whole new set of tools with a whole new toolbox. This is exciting stuff. It might feel scary and you might not know how or where to start, and that's OK. You've already come a long way by reading this book. The next step is to commit to change. And then below you will find a whole bunch of ideas and action points to take to keep you on course.

What do you do now?

I stared at the screen for a long time before I was able to write this section. What I decided to do was ask myself this question. If I was a reader of this book right now what would I do next? And so, I am just going to bullet point a bunch of things that I would do if I were you, the reader. Here goes:

1. I would interview the salesperson of the company's 5 biggest digital accounts to find out these things

    a. How did we land the account?
    b. How long have they been doing business with us?
    c. What do they buy from us and why?

2. I would develop my vertical market targets based on the success of both my own accounts and the largest accounts the company has.

3. I would sit down with the owner of the company and have him/her tell me 4-5 examples of digital projects that we are the best at, along with the company's competitive advantage.

4. I would look around the internet to try to find some really great case studies of digital printing today. It took me about 3 minutes to find these three sources:

    a. http://www.podi.org/
    b. http://printinthemix.com/
    c. https://www.msp-pgh.com/assets/podi_pearl.pdf

5. I would research every client I have and determine where and how they are using social media. I would then make sure that I have a professional presence everywhere I found clients. This will be at a minimum LinkedIn, Twitter and Facebook, and probably Pinterest and Instagram as well.

7. I would commit to spending time with all of these channels every day and set goals for myself for cultivating followers.

8. I would make a list of people out there who are sharing and creating great content.

9. I would create a schedule for each channel and what content I am sharing on each one.

    a. Sharing is caring. It is perfectly OK if all you do is re-tweet and share cool stuff that you find. Here are some cool examples of places to find great content

        i. For Print Only

        ii. Ink On Da Paper

        iii. What They Think

        iv. PrintMediaCentr

        v. Branding Strategy Insider

        vi. Marketing Profs

        vii. Inc

        viii. Harvard Business Review

        ix. Fast Company

        x. Seth Godin

    b. You can get remarkable results using your social presence in as little as 5 minutes per day per channel. You could just decide that the first thing you are going to day each day is sit down at your desk with your morning coffee and get your social on. The surprise byproduct is that you will learn something new every day, and you will have fun and will become the kind of person that is never short of conversation in a group setting because you have always "just read the most interesting article." And it will always be true.

10. I would become the kind of person who is obsessed with finding the right fit. Every message, every phone

call, every letter, every post, must be about finding the people out there who are open to learning something new; who are open to change. You are now the person who will teach them, inform them, and help them see that there is more than one way. And your way just might be the better way. But this way is gentler; it is less aggressive. This way does not ask, "What's in it for me?" This way knows that the sales will come to you because of your approach. Your way builds trust. Your way conveys credibility. Your way lets them know that you are ready to work with them at no time other than when they are ready to make a change because it benefits them.

A lot of this might feel counter-intuitive to you. It might not be what you learned when you got started X years ago. That's OK. As we said at the top, digital is different. The people that you are trying to engage with are different. So, it makes sense then that you would use a different approach with different tools.

If you've seen the movie *Jerry Maguire*, you'll remember that Jerry had an epiphany one night in which he realized that he wanted to do business in a different way than all of his cohorts. He wanted to pay more attention to his clients and give them more personal service. In some ways we are saying the same thing. It doesn't make sense to sell to people in a way that does not feel comfortable for you. You must be authentic. Be yourself. Allow yourself to be known and understood by those you are seeking to work with. You will reap the rewards. Maybe not immediately, but you will. Remember Jerry? It took the whole season for his philosophy to pay off. But, it ultimately did. Big time.

Kelly Mallozzi
773-680-5134
kelly@successinprint.net

Bill's turn...

Two thoughts for the owner:

1. Years ago, I worked with a client named Sean Fitzgerald. Sean was a former digital press operator who made the difficult leap into sales. On one of our first coaching conversations I asked him to summarize his new role. If Sean were given a $1 royalty for every time I have repeated his answer, he could be retired. He said, "We help our customers to find their customers." The customer. It's all about the customer. Every time I find myself asking the question, "Where should I take my business next?" I remember that it's my clients who have the answer. If you are an owner thinking about getting into digital/inkjet print, your answers lie with your customers. Start there. Find out where they are going. Ask what their challenges are. Don't buy digital/inkjet printing equipment because you're getting a great deal. Don't buy it because your competitors all have it. Go digital when the customer leads you there.

2. The Number One conversation that I get into— by far— has to do with finding salespeople. "No one wants to sell print." "There aren't any good salespeople out there." If this is an issue for commercial print, it's more so regarding digital/inkjet. Owners struggle in part because they are applying time-tested recruiting strategies to a changed printing industry. Say what you want about Bill Belichick, the head coach of the New England Patriots, but the guy has built a system that results in AFC Championships and a Super Bowl ring for every finger on Tom Brady's hand. You, my dear owner, must rethink your system first before you go out and look for salespeople. Build a marketing campaign. Create the lead generation system. See to it that once a sales rep brings in an order,

Production takes over and that's the last time he or she is involved in the process. In short, let the salespeople sell. By removing sales responsibilities on the front and back ends, the skill set you are looking for in the salesperson (hunter, prospector, bush-beater) means the pool of talent to choose from has become considerably larger. The pace of sales, life, and business has quickened. Digital/inkjet is a perfect example. Get your house in order first and only then should you be seeking a rep.

And two for the sales reps:

1. Look, if you want to keep your head in the sand and not sell digital/inkjet, I sincerely hope you are 64 years old with a 401(k) earning double digits. If not, face your fears and rethink your arguments against the technology. It's a teachable skill, BUT you need open ears and a willing attitude. Do you remember why you got into sales in the first place? Part of the reason was probably to solve problems and be creative. So, when's the last time you did that? If you think to yourself, "My clients love me," you are in trouble. They will leave you and you won't see it coming. If you aren't scared of losing business, you should be (in part, because Kelly and I are constantly training hungry reps to kick ass on complacent salespeople and to take their accounts away with ideas and sales techniques that you once engaged).

2. The best overall advice I can give you is to stay sales curious. Be aware of the opportunities all around you. They're there. You just need to look for them, starting in your own life. What are you an expert in? What are your interests and experiences? For example, the Addendum of this book includes information about selling to Colleges. I've gone through the college admissions pro-

cess with each of my three girls. I get it. I can sell to it. I was brought up Episcopalian, not only Sundays but all week long, as my dad was the Treasurer for the Diocese in Massachusetts. This gave me keen insight and interest into that world and, subsequently, was written up as another vertical market opportunity. Sales is the best job in the world. Where else do you get to solve a problem with a creative solution you came up with and then see it put into action? See digital/inkjet as an annoying toddler and you are missing an amazingly fun and lucrative opportunity. See it as your future and you open up a new world of possibility. The first step is to see that world with open eyes!

Bill Farquharson
781-934-7036
bill@aspirefor.com

From us both:

We hope these ideas have been valuable to you. Some of it might have been obvious, and some of it thought-provoking new territory that you hadn't considered. The idea was to get you prepared for success in digital/inkjet. Having first sold it and then created seemingly endless amounts of training content, we can assure you that while digital is another tool in the toolbox, it's not just another tool in the toolbox. Treat it like every other piece of equipment and you are missing an opportunity. Digital/inkjet changes everything. Let the fun begin.

We are dedicated to your success—here in this book and beyond. Please do reach out if we can further assist you or your sales team.

Bill and Kelly

ADDENDUM

"Who's Making Money?"
Verticals: A Sales Primer

"Who's Making Money?"
Verticals: A Sales Primer

This final section will cover the subject of digital/inkjet sales, but strictly as it relates to vertical markets. (Warning: This assumes you already know how to sell. Our conversation is about the verticals best suited for digital/inkjet print). In case it is an unfamiliar term, a vertical market is a particular industry, like banking or healthcare, and all of the companies and organizations that compete and do business within that vertical.

The value of focusing on one particular vertical market comes over time. Most every company or organization within a particular vertical faces the same business needs and challenges. While the very first call might be difficult, things become exponentially easier on the second, third, and fourth calls after that as you better learn the questions to ask and know the likely replies. Your credibility will skyrocket when it becomes clear to the prospect that you understand their business. We've tried to select some of the more popular vertical markets for you to sell into. But before we get to them, we'll provide some sales fundamentals so we're all on the same page. We begin with a quick sales lesson or two. We've been shamelessly promoting Bill's other book and pointing you to Amazon, but this time we'll steal a few of his key points...

If sales could be broken down into four basic elements, they would be:

1. Make a high value, well-researched sales call;
2. Call on the best prospects possible;
3. Engage in a step-by-step prospecting process;
4. Apply diligence and pleasant persistence.

Let's take a look at each...

Making a high value sales call

If a sales trainer were allowed to only teach one skill, it would be that of understanding precisely what to say during the prospecting process. The preparation and planning that comes prior to picking up the phone for the first time or sending that first email makes all the difference. Having something of value to say not only improves the quality of the sales call, but also the confidence with which the call is made. Even the voicemail messages left are better.

When it comes to call quality, the bottom rung in the ladder sounds like this: "Do you have anything that I can quote on?" A sales call that begins that way can only have one ending: "Sorry but your price is too high." With this approach, business can only be won by having the lowest number. In a high value, well-researched sales call, business is earned by presenting a good idea, one that lowers the usage cost of the document or increases its value (remember the lesson from earlier in this book: Solve the problem, earn the order). The starting point for this better sales call is the investigation into the business needs of the company or organization. Recall the lesson from Dale Carnegie's "How to Win Friends and Influence People:" You can get what you want when you figure out what the other guy wants and then help him to get it. And just what does virtually every company and organization want? Growth! Revenue! Sales!

Consider this: There are only three ways to grow (other than mergers and acquisitions, that is):

- Find more customers;
- Sell more to existing customers;
- Go into entirely new markets and serve an entirely different customer base.

Applying Carnegie's lesson then, if you can figure out which one or more of these growth strategies is being applied/attempted by a prospect and you have an idea that can help them achieve growth, you can earn their business without competing on price at all.

Calling on the best prospects

Calling on the best prospects possible seems like a no-brainer. Isn't that obvious? Yes, of course it is. But the trick is knowing where to look to find them. One way to look at this is from the standpoint of the company that you work for. What makes for a great fit for one printer would be a terrible idea for another. And then there's the target market of the individual salespeople. Two salespeople of different genders, in different generations, are naturally going to have two different sweet spots when it comes to calling on the best prospects. The only common denominator is how they go about looking for their new business opportunities. They can buy a list, search the internet or they could simply pursue a vertical market. And that is ultimately what this section is about!

Engaging in a step-by-step prospecting process

Similar to advertising, a sale is the result of a message repeated multiple times and over multiple mediums. Success comes in the form of an appointment and is the result of a step-by-step, week-by-week prospecting process. The good news is, there is no one single process that works for everyone all the time. To the contrary, the exact same plan can be applied by multiple salespeople in different parts of the country and each can achieve a different outcome. What's important is the consistency with which the process is applied. That's where the money is.

Diligence and pleasant persistence

Finally, comes diligence and pleasant persistence. This step can be summarized as follows:

- Make the calls
- Make the calls, and, oh yeah…
- Make the calls.

Great! With that foundation in mind, let's move to the template we used to approach each vertical market:

1. First, understand the vertical in advance from a business standpoint. That is, what are their business needs, rather than print needs? This means doing research to the point where you are a subject matter expert (SME). What are their challenges? What are their threats? What are the industry trends? What are their options for growing revenue? Perhaps you could find a company/organization in that vertical to call on and get firsthand information. Research it. Find the problem(s) that digital/inkjet printing solves. The endgame is to have an ending to the sentence that begins, "The purpose of my call is…", one that points to the research you have done on that particular company/ organization and your overall knowledge of the vertical itself.

2. Next, find out who you want to talk to about that issue you have uncovered. This might be as simple as looking up the company on LinkedIn.

3. For the third step, you'll need a pad of paper and a pen. Imagine yourself sitting with the person from Step B. What questions would you ask in order to get more information? Write them down.

4. Finally, apply your step-by-step, week-by-week prospecting process with diligence and pleasant persistency.

Okay! Now that we have our primer in sales behind us, let's focus on five vertical markets and apply these lessons in the following areas:

- Banks/Credit Unions
- Hospitals/Medical Centers
- Colleges/Universities and Secondary Schools
- Restaurants
- Non-Profits

Each vertical market covers:

1. **Primary Business Needs**—We start by discussing how each vertical drives revenue. Remember, you can get what you want (a digital/inkjet printing sale!) when you help them get what they want (growth!);

2. **General, Background Information**—From our extensive research, we'll make you Subject Matter Experts in no time. These details might not hit you as game-changers, but mention them in conversation with a prospect and your credibility will skyrocket;

3. **Opportunities for Digital/Inkjet and Key Contacts**—Next, we spell out what we believe to be the best places to apply digital/inkjet printing solutions and include where to look for the contact points. You're welcome;

4. **The Conversation**—Questions to ask, possible sales objections, and your response

5. **Additional resources** (videos, links, research suggestions)

Again, your goal is not to win orders based on providing a lower price, but rather earn their business by offering up a better idea to help them to achieve their goals. To do this, you must have a broad and in-depth understanding of the business challenges faced by companies/organizations within the specific vertical.

Knowledge is power, gang. You gain immense credibility when you display knowledge of the challenges faced by a company/organization, knowledge that is revealed in the following pages.

Ready? Great. Let's do this...

Vertical Markets
#1 Banks and Credit Unions

Selling Digital/Inkjet to Banks and Credit Unions

We lump Banks and Credit Unions together, although they could not be more different. Only recently have Banks shown any interest or need in advertising and marketing. What was once a small town, get-a-toaster-for-opening-a-checking-account, "everybody knows your name" kind of business has become Corporate, faceless and branded. They have an image problem and a challenge to grow. Technology has shaken the vertical to the core, with millennials rejecting the standard model and banking online. Now, a regional bank can be national and even international due to the accessibility of financial transactions online and through hand-held devices. It is almost impossible for a single-site bank to succeed today. Still, the fundamentals remain and one of them is to find new depositors. In that department, as you will read below, free toasters have been replaced.

Primary Business Needs

Get More Customers—You don't have to look too far to find a Bank's marketing campaign for ongoing promotions. They typically have a central theme/message as they try to build a brand and woo new customers, stealing them from other institutions. Making it difficult to switch, however, is the fact that many of us use our bank's electronic banking solutions to pay bills. Changing banks means setting everything up with our new choice, entering the contact information, remittance addresses, and account numbers all over again. This fact makes it imperative that Banks successfully convince their customer bases to connect in this manner and use the online banking options to help lock them in. By the time the marketing campaign is announced, it is likely too late for you to help. But still, by studying the campaign (and you might consider hitting the "Contact Us" link and requesting information) you can at least make contact to find out the results.

Banks use print as a way to drive demand for their products and services and especially to solicit new deposits through poaching their competitors. According to an article in the Wall Street Journal (June 23/24, 2018) Weekend Edition), "deposit bonuses" are more common. Here, banks reward new customers with $200-300 when checking accounts are opened and maintained for 90 days (minimum balances are typically $5,000+). From the article: "Over the six months ended in March 2018, the number of banks sending more than five million of the mail offers has risen to 15 from seven in mid-2015."

A second poaching tactic is to offer refinancing of cars and student loans. Do you remember that example we gave way back in Section One? It was about the banner hanging from the rafters: "Refinance your car here. Save money with our 3.99% rate." Again, print had a role.

Earn Greater Share of Customer— Once upon a time, Banks made their money by taking Peter's deposit and loaning it to Paul. Peter was given X percent interest and Paul was charged Y percent, and the bank profited from the difference. Today, their financial portfolios include everything from basic loans to retirement plans and even straying into new markets, making it necessary for the bank to communicate their wide array of products and services.

Offer New "Products," to New Markets— Banks are heavily regulated, so they are not allowed to offer new services without permission. But, occasionally, as was the case a few years back when Massachusetts banks were allowed to sell life insurance, they service an entirely different target market.

General Information and Digital/Inkjet Selling Opportunities:

That Wall Street Journal article regarding deposit bonuses offers an interesting opportunity. Find this article at WSJ.com (June 23, 2018: "These Bank Customers are Making a Bundle on Their Deposits") and use it as part of a prospecting process. Your sales pitch is made significantly easier when following up, since you have something concrete to discuss. Could you do something similar for them? The Key Contacts for your sales pitch would be Marketing, President, and C Level.

Banks continue to have an image problem. The 2009 financial crisis was the undoing of the trust they once enjoyed. Then, after the bailout, misuse of customers' personal information further soured public opinion. An executive at Wellesley Bank (Massachusetts) told Bill that a survey revealed 80% of customers hate their bank. Not dislike. HATE. They were shocked. Gone is the personal touch, no matter what they say, and relationships mean less when it comes to offering credit. This problem is only getting worse as people use online accounts to perform most banking transactions. This is shuttering brick-and-mortar offices and further de-personalizing banks from their customers. Banks counter this issue by rallying around a cause, sponsoring events, or supporting local charities. The bank's website should be the first place to look for information on what they are supporting. Banks spend 10 times as much money on sponsorships than they do on marketing. You will find their name associated with local events and charities (look especially in local newspapers—and especially the weekend edition—for everything from concerts to fairs and various nonprofit events). An added sales benefit is that it also opens up the opportunity to gain access to the companies and corporations that are also sponsoring those events.

Opportunity #1: Philanthropic Endeavors

You can help! Call attention to the bank's philanthropic endeavors and help rebuild their image using digital/inkjet mailings, fliers, and wide format output.

Key Contacts: Marketing, President, C Level, Purchasing or someone at their Foundation. In addition, press releases announcing local events typically have a quote from a bank contact.

Research: Look first to their website. It might be as blatant as a "Sponsorship" or "Foundation" tab. Look also to their "News" section. Second, look to Google for current and past events the bank or credit union might have had their name associated with.

Your Opening Pitch: "The purpose of my call is to talk about how I can help the bank build its brand through the various events and causes it sponsors. For example..." (refer to your research).

The Questions to Ask:
- "How is success measured when sponsoring an event?"
- "How do you choose which events or charities to sponsor?"

- "What has the bank done in the past to get the word out?"
- "From the standpoint of promoting an event, what is typically involved: Mailings, fliers, banners, etc.?"
- "What does 'ideal' look like to you?"

Final thought on this Opportunity: Here's a wild idea: For the cost of a donated banner ($200-$300), you could get access to potentially dozens of sponsors' Marketing departments since you would need their logos to print the piece. Not a bad ROI.

Opportunity #2: Event Promotion

Banks and Credit Unions do a fair amount of educational events as a way of promoting their various products and services. Information is found on the website.

Opportunity: Help promote these events using your digital/inkjet capabilities. Postcards for mailing, fliers, announcement sheets, wide-format banners before the event. Then wide-format at the event. You might even help them handle the data collected from attendees for follow-up. Similar to trade shows, event organizers often drop the ball by delaying follow-up action on the leads generated.

Key Contacts and Research: Check the website (look under "Upcoming Events" or "Calendar". There might also be a Press Release) or LinkedIn for the names of those in charge of local events.

Your Opening Pitch: "The purpose of my call is to speak with about ways I can help the bank promote the events you have posted on your website."

The Questions to Ask:

- "What has the bank done in the past?"
- "What is the status of your data base?"
- "Do you ever hold private events at a company?"
- "What is the follow up protocol AND do you know if it is being followed?"

Everything that is revealed here regarding Banks holds true for Credit Unions. The difference is that Credit Unions are smaller, meaning contact information (Decision-Makers) is easier to find and they are in more need of your help. There are print and marketing companies that specialize in helping Credit Unions to market themselves. That's all they do. This should tell you something about the opportunity this vertical presents.

Credit Unions are the ugly stepsister of the financial world. They are more like a banking club than anything else and typically have their origins associated with a group (American Airlines Federal Credit Union, for example). They are governed and taxed differently, and often offer better interest rates. However, since they do such a poor job of getting the word out, they lag well behind banks. Note: One point of difference is the language they use, often calling their depositers "members" instead of "customers."

Opportunity #3: Communicating Offers & Rates

Use the power of digital/inkjet printing to communicate a credit union's offerings and rates. Similar to banks, CU's need help gaining new depositors. Perhaps you could suggest an incentive offered though a mailing, customized to the individual.

Key contacts: Local branch managers are a good place to start. Then, Presidents and Regional Managers.

Research: Look to your own mailbox and ask around to see if anyone can recall hearing from this CU about their offerings. Look at their website and pay particular attention to the brand they are pushing as well as any marketing push currently in play.

Your Opening Pitch: "The purpose of my call is to talk about how I can help bring in new members using the various capabilities my company has to offer."

The Questions to Ask:

- "What is the status of your current promotion? Have you seen any results yet?"
- "Who is your target market?"
- "How do people find you now?"
- "What is your Credit Union's differentiator?"
- "Who do you consider your competition?"
- "Overall, is the emphasis on attracting new customers or getting more from existing customers?"
- "What is your Credit Union's current use of print?"
- "What is the status of your database?"

Opportunity #4: Sell More to Current Customers

Similar to other businesses, banks make their money by getting the most out of each customer. They want to make sure that you are taking advantage of their full (and constantly increasing) range of products and services. The challenge is to get the word out on what's available. Banks need to engage people in a conversation, either face-to-face or over the phone. Websites can advertise, but it's only when some personal form of conversation happens that a "sale" is made.

Opportunity: If you have variable data printing capabilities, you can help banks identify groups within its client base who use only one of their services to take advantage of more that the bank offers. This might be one of the occasions you'll hear the objection, "We don't print as much. We do everything online." To counter this, point out that digital/inkjet printing can drive customers to the website and augment other marketing efforts.

Key contacts: Marketing, Purchasing, IT Director

Research: The bank's website will tell you what is currently being emphasized, but that should only be used as a reference point as a way of gaining credibility for having done some homework ahead of time. Make a list of the array of services the bank offers and have it handy when you call.

Your Opening Pitch: "The purpose of my call is to talk to you about how I can help you get greater share of customer."

The Questions to Ask:
- "What have you done in the past to cross-promote the bank's services and how effective has it been?"
- "What is the status of your database? Is it divided up by 'product offering?'"

A common objection will be that you are not a client of that bank. Tough one to beat. We have long believed that a good idea is enough to overcome this issue. You might ask before you offer up any suggestions that could be taken to your competition.

Opportunity #5: Promote Cybersecurity

A big issue for banks these days is cybersecurity. Customers need reassurance that their money is safe and secure as well as tips for doing their part in reducing the risk for a hack. Banks are constantly getting these messages out. When a breach does occur, there are protocols in place that might include digital/inkjet printing for communication purposes and PR. Speed is a key factor in the sale here.

Opportunity: Prepare a program that helps with damage control in the event of a security breach. If you had a template for handling a client disaster and let the Banks know of its existence, it would only be a matter of time before your phone rang. At that point, there is no price objection!

Key contacts: Straight to the top on this one—President, CEO. The website or LinkedIn might also list a job title having to do with cyber security.

Research: Look into the damage done (both financially and to the reputation of the institution) when a breach occurs and list examples, especially the more high-profile cases that will ring a bell (Hello, Wells Fargo?) as a wake-up call to anyone you speak with not up on the potential for disaster.

Your Opening Pitch: "The purpose of my call is to help establish a protocol to follow in the event of a data breach. My company can help with customer communications in times of emergencies."

The Questions to Ask:
- "What preparations are currently in place?"
- "How important is speed in communicating to customers in a situation such as this?"

Some banks deal in Commercial Real Estate. The salespeople in these departments are often contractors or are employees paid on commission and have full buying authority. You might want to make contact directly here as they could very well purchase their own signage.

It might be tempting for you to go after the Buyer or the Marketing Department, if a bank headquarters location has one, as a first step. Don't do that. Instead, start at your own local bank and with your branch Bank Manager so that you can learn in a comfortable, more accessible environment. You are a customer of theirs, so turn to the local manager as a key source of valuable information. Sit with him/her and talk about the business side of the bank. Find out what the promotion du jour is (Banks are always focusing on one specific part of their financial portfolio of services) and who is in charge of it. The Manager has likely been briefed on what the offer is but, more importantly, can give you a street-level view of how well it is working and how it might be improved. This is valuable information that can be used in a sales call, so be sure to find out the name of the person to call and even go so far as to ask the Manager for an introduction.

Additional Resources

Ongoing: Put in extensive time studying this vertical so that you understand current events, back stories, existing challenges, and future opportunities. Two suggestions: First, google "10 Marketing Mistakes Banks Make" and read some incredibly valuable background information and talking points to be brought up during your prospecting approach. Second, *The Wall Street Journal* covers this industry almost daily. If you are a subscriber (and if not, why not???), start paying attention. You can also get this information online via its website, www.WSJ.com.

We also recommend you marinate in the minutia of the banking world by reading "Deloitte's 2018 Banking Outlook," which you'll easily find on Google. While lengthy and needlessly technical, it does provide some information that will fill in the blanks should this vertical market be a major opportunity for you. For example, "Banks need to rebuild around digital" and "Differentiation can be found through technology adoption." There are some key talking points to be had.

Interested in a video on selling to banks? Send Bill an email bill@ aspirefor.com and he will forward a link.

VERTICAL MARKETS
#2 Hospitals and Medical Centers

Selling Digital/Inkjet to Hospitals and Medical Centers

Another vertical market most people are familiar with is the hospital industry and, along with it, local medical centers (including strip mall walk-ins and drugstore clinics, a.k.a. "Doc in a box." This vertical seems to be in constant transition as laws, insurance companies, and the aging population make for a never-ending need to evolve. Let's start with some a discussion of their growth strategies:

Primary Business Needs

Get More Patients—In theory, a hospital's business plan would be to attract new patients and then attempt to service them throughout life's stages. Privacy laws make that difficult, however, as the use of patient information is strictly verboten in most situations. Gaining new "customers," then, comes from two main areas: Doctor referrals and patient choice due to either reputation or location. Considerable money is spent on print and online to market a specific brand, emphasizing a hospital's capabilities, expertise, and/or reputation. This is an ongoing process that, for larger institutions, involves an ad agency. Be sure to do your homework prior to the start of any prospecting process involving a hospital or medical center.

Earn Greater Share of Customer—In recent years, hospitals have been experimenting with patient loyalty programs, giving rewards for repeat business and referrals. Similar to airlines, points are given and awards can result. There have been mixed results and mixed reaction. In general, a hospital wants Bill's thumb surgery when he learned that 6'6" men should not snowboard, his rotator cuff repair when his misspent youth caught up to him, and the a-fib heart surgery so that he can play bad golf without a racing heartbeat. As he and other middle-aged men age, his local hospital should remind him of the care options. He is, to put it one way, an annuity. Oh, and he also twisted his ankle badly enough to require a trip to the Emergency Room. See? This guy is a one-man profit center! Imagine the lifetime value he represents to them as an aging and active male. From a business standpoint, the hospital should be inundating him with information so they stay top of mind the next time he forgets that he's no longer 25 years old. Make sense?

Offer New "Products," to New Markets—Innovation in medical science often opens up completely new opportunities for growth. MRI's, for example, became widespread in the early 1980s and hospitals everywhere opened up new departments. As you will see below, advances continue. Sometimes it's a new technology while other times it's merely a change in geography.

General Information and Digital/Inkjet Selling Opportunities:

The upside: Regardless of economic conditions, the Medical Industry seems to plod along and remains a great vertical market to approach, one that is almost impervious to external forces. There's lots of money there. We could probably write forever on the subject since there are so many different facets, but we'll settle for giving just enough information so that you can seek the right kind of conversations.

The downside: There are a number of buying groups, as well as a fair amount of chaos and disorder. Hospitals, in some cases, are not very well-run from a business sense and purchasing power is not always clear. Sometimes purchasing is centralized and other times just the opposite. You very well may need GPS to find your way around this maze!

The best way to view Hospitals is to look at them as being made up of smaller profit centers. Each department within the Hospital— Maternity, MRI/X-Ray, Emergency, Cancer, etc.— is like an individual business. They all need to turn a profit and, in most cases, there is someone in charge of that task within the department—someone whose income might also be partially dependent on its success. Example: Years ago, one facility outside of Boston, Newton-Wellesley Hospital, redecorated its maternity ward to the point that it looked more like a Marriott Hotel. Then, it undertook a massive advertising campaign in an attempt to get its target market— young, affluent couples— to deliver their babies in style. Such an approach was unheard of at the time. Now, it is commonplace.

Opportunity #1: Promote Service Offerings

Help the hospital to make a success out of its various service offerings.

Key Contacts: Your goal is to find out who is in charge of making any given department profitable and then getting in front of him/her and learning more.

Research: A hospital's website will tell you what they are promoting. It might be a specific department or a theme/brand as a whole. Look especially at press releases for information, announcements, and contact names.

Your Opening Pitch: "The purpose of my call is to help you make your department successful and profitable."

The Questions to Ask:

- "Why do people choose your hospital?"
- "How do new patients who come to your department/hospital find you? Are they referred by their physician or do they choose you based on another factor, such as external marketing?"
- "What is your differentiator?"
- "What brand message are you communicating?"
- "What marketing have you done in the past?"
- "How has its effectiveness been measured?"
- "What effort do you/can you do to let doctors in the area know about your capabilities in order to gather additional patient referrals from them?"
- What is your current approach to getting people to try your department for the first time?"
- "Who is your target market?"
- "What do you consider to be the Number One reason why people try your department/hospital for the first time?"
- "Tell me about your database. Is it up-to-date and accurate? You are certainly restricted as to how you can use the information, but what, if anything, have you done from a marketing standpoint?"
- "Is your business seasonal or cyclical in any way?"
- "Who is your competition?"
- "Does the hospital have any outlying locations, such as clinics or a standalone Emergency Center?"

We strongly suggest you visit the hospital(s) that you are targeting and walk around, perhaps taking pictures of the signage you see, as well as to gather any printed material that may be lying around. This will help give you a feel for the facility and provide information that you might refer to later. If you take this advice, take special notice of the wide-format printing opportunities and especially any corporate sponsorship (look for logos on banners). You might kill two birds with one sales stone and gain access to other companies.

Hospitals are, by nature, political and complex from a business standpoint. It's important to find out what kind of buying authority exists outside of Purchasing. We always believe that a good idea will ultimately find its audience and will be rewarded with a sale. However, it might also come down to a bid. As a result, find out what opportunities exist early so that you are not wasting your time. While a difficult task, it is not an impossible one. A robust LinkedIn presence will give you a large enough network of contacts to find someone willing to give you the inside skinny on how things work.

Hospitals have plenty of competition, and not just from other hospitals. This makes patient retention a hot issue. They want your next procedure, your next operation. Binding their hands on this issue are the HPPA privacy laws, but that doesn't stop hospitals from trying. This is a higher-level conversation, one to be had with upper management. Here are a few Questions to Ask that might be helpful:

- "What percentage of your business is repeat?"
- "How do you use your mailing list/database?"
- "Does your department/hospital do any kind of patient follow-up?"
- "What do you currently do to get people to return a second time?"

- "What do you do to collect data on your existing customers?"
- "What do you currently do to create a relationship, that is, start a dialogue with your patient base?"

While hospitals offer myriad opportunities and have huge potential, they are political, inefficient, and can rely on years-long buying contracts that lock out the non-incumbent vendor. As such, attempting to sell by going through the front door (Purchasing, bids, RFQ's, etc.) doesn't sound terribly appealing to us. We recommend you try a side door: Hospitals events, such as fundraisers and auctions. Donations of print might get you an invite. There, you can hobnob with hospital brass and meet some key contacts. The other thought is to check out the training event list on the website and help build their success. Then, network your way around the building. It's not a fast sale, but neither is waiting for a print contract to end.

Opportunity #2: Promote Events

Research and Key Contacts: Scour the website for information on upcoming events. In addition, use Google to learn the timing of major fundraisers in the past. Many of these events are annual. On that subject, also look for event planners who boast that the hospital is a client. Perhaps it is they who you want to contact. Whether you donate digital/inkjet printing or simply offer to help with an event's success, you are likely to find a more easily-accessible contact.

The Questions to Ask:
- "How are you promoting each event?"
- "What have you done in the past and what has been successful?"
- "Who is the target market for this event?"
- "What is the follow-up protocol?"

- "Do you provide any kind of training or education locally?"
- "Do you hold any kind of charity or community events?"

Another trend in this vertical has to do with care facilities that are typically found in retail shopping centers. These so-called "Doc-in-a-box" locations target patients who lack a primary physician and/or the non-trauma walk-in customer who might need care for a minor injury or something like the flu and prefers the convenience. Some of these facilities are connected to and run by a Hospital, while others are independent.

Your best bet in this situation is to visit one in-person or go online and investigate. Bring your next case of the sniffles here and learn all that you can. This "level" of care is itself a profit center because business is being steered away from doctor's offices. Follow-up mailings and periodic reminders of their services make this a nice annuity for you.

On February 26, 2018, the Wall Street Journal published a special report on healthcare that we urge you to find and read thoroughly. They looked at the overall economics and trends of the industry and made several observations:

New hospitals are getting smaller;

Healthcare providers are investing in outpatient clinics, same-day surgery centers, freestanding emergency rooms, and micro hospitals that offer as few as eight beds for overnight stays;*

Digital technology has allowed hospitals to monitor people at home after their stay;
All of this is driven by simple economics: Traditional hospital care is too costly and inefficient for many medical issues.

All of this change must be communicated to the patients and the general public. That's where you come in.

*To counter that money-grab, insurers have started pushing back by denying claims for "Avoidable" emergency room visits (see New York Times article, May 20, 2018). It's this kind of chess game that is well-documented and requires your constant review if you want more than just a chance to quote.

Finally, major pharmacy chains, such as CVS and Walgreens, are installing care facilities that are one step down from the retail care centers and handle only colds and flu-level diagnosis. The advantage here is obvious: Treat them at the pharmacy and they will then buy the remedies from the pharmacy. This is a growing trend in the medical industry.

Typical Sales Objections and a Final Thought

Because hospitals are notoriously poorly run from a business sense, we suspect that your selling cycle will be longer and will have to include more education than usual. Other than the Hospital Administrator, formal business training is not part of the typical employee's background. This means that the typical objection coming from Hospitals will be less focused on price and more so on process and procedure. Believe it or not, you will hear a lot of, "that won't work here," in deference to the difficulty that you'll encounter in trying to change mindsets.

Additional Resources

The Wall Street Journal—Because hospitals are such big business and healthcare is a major concern for companies and individuals, the Journal runs frequent stories regarding trends. From time to time they even run a Special Report pull-out section, such as the Feb. 25, 2018, piece called "What the Hospital of the Future Looks Like."

Interested in a video on selling to Hospitals? Send Bill an email (bill@aspirefor.com) and he will forward a link.

We strongly suggest you Google, "10 Marketing Mistakes Hospitals Make" as it will give you a plethora of background information and ideas, leading to credibility.

VERTICAL MARKETS
#3 Churches

Selling Digital/Inkjet to Churches

Depending where you live in the country, churches are big business, some even of biblical proportions (see what we did there?). As such, big opportunities exist.

Primary Business Needs

The primary business needs model of business—more customers, more from existing customers, new markets—does not completely translate to this vertical market. There isn't much fit for "Greater share of customer" or "New products/New markets." Churches have business needs, but each has a different spin:

1. **Increase membership**—All churches have the constant need to grow and engage their congregation. Note that these two separate functions are not dissimilar from a business: They are seeking new members and looking to get more engagement from existing members; They want to convert occasional, holiday visitors to members;
2. **Stewardship**—The annual practice of securing a financial basis of regular contributors;
3. **The occasional capital campaign**—This is typically done every 3-7 years and has a specific purpose in mind, such as an expansion or upkeep of existing property (church building or parsonage);

4. **Special Events**—From time to time, churches have one-off meetings or educational programs that require promotion

General Information and Digital/Inkjet Selling Opportunities

Churches generally operate on a calendar year, one that does not necessarily start in January. One religion, as Robin Williams comically pointed out, is even color-coded ("Ten best things about being an Episcopalian"...great YouTube video). Unofficially, there are "seasons" to each church, typically coinciding with the school year. That is, people will go back to church at about the same time their kids return to classes. It represents an opportunity for a church to grow its numbers since many people join a church to expose their children to religion. This also represents a sales engagement opportunity for you. Be aware of this and you can time your prospecting to take advantage of the different spikes.

Opportunity #1: Increase Membership

In May or June, put together a marketing campaign that addresses this "Back to School/Back to Church" membership drive. Either make direct sales calls or start your sales process with a flier that lists a price and then what it buys you (i.e.: "For $499, you get two banners and four posters in full-color!" or perhaps a combination of banners, posters, mailing, and fliers—all printed digitally or with your inkjet printer).

Key Contacts: Church staff, Pastor, or Director of Christian Education.

Research: Their website will give you information on upcoming events, including any "Back to Church"-style dates. Depending on the time of year you are doing your search, you might need to look back at previous years to learn what they do and when.

Your Opening Pitch: "The purpose of my call is to help the church attract new members to your congregation."

The Questions to Ask:

- "What is your current approach to growing your congregation?"
- How effective has that been? Any measured results?"
- "How do new members currently find your church?"
- "Who is your target market? That is, does your church have an ideal type of member, such as a family, newly married couple or a young single person?"
- "What do you consider to be the Number One reason why people join your church?"
- "Tell me about your database. Is it up-to-date and accurate?"
- "Do you have any kind of 'Back to Church' events?"
- "Let's talk about the Christian holidays. What does the church do to capture contact information of those parishioners/people who show up only at Christmas and Easter?"

Opportunity #2: Stewardship

And then there's Stewardship. Churches survive financially on a combination of annual pledges, one-time donations, the collection plate, legacy gifts, and income from investments. Each year, most churches have a pledge drive known as a "Stewardship Campaign." This is typically done in the fall during fundraising season (what, did you think the rush of pre-Thanksgiving appeal letters you get were anything but timed for the holidays?). Annual donation commitments form the core of a church's revenue and budgets for the new year are based on the results. In short, there's a lot riding on this.

No one goes to school to learn how to hold a successful Stewardship Campaign. For the typical church, it's "What did we do last year? Let's do that again." Speeches are given from the pulpit over a series of Sundays (mostly from parishioners). A deadline is set. Pledge letters go out. Phone call follow ups are made. And that's it. How'd we do? You can help.

Key Contacts: There is likely a volunteer committee taking the lead on this. Chances are the group that did it last year has left and a new team (open to new ideas) now holds the reins. You might find names on the website but more likely a call to the church office will yield a contact target.

Research: Most church websites will provide information regarding the timing of a stewardship campaign. Note that this is different from a "Click here to give" one-off donation opportunity. You'd be wise to also look at, "How to run an effective stewardship campaign" on The Google for some background information.

Your Opening Pitch: "The purpose of my call is to help the church with its Stewardship Campaign. There are many ways to communicate and the congregation might need the message sent using different mediums and methods."

The Questions to Ask:
- "What time of year do you typically run your stewardship campaigns?"
- "In the past, what have you done and how effective has it been?"
- "Tell me about your database. Is it up-to-date and accurate?"

Opportunity #3: Convert Occasional Visitors to Members

There are two major Christian holidays—Christmas and Easter—that tend to bring the occasional church-goers into the pews. Churches try to take advantage of this and convert them to be regulars.

Printed material with specific messages (read: Versioning) from your digital/inkjet press would make for a nice suggestion. In addition, you could help them capture personal information for use with follow-up mailings.

Key Contacts: Church staff or Pastor.

Your Opening Pitch: "The purpose of my call is to help capture the contact information of the church's occasional visitors for the purpose of follow up so that we can make them active members of the congregation."

The Questions to Ask:
- "What, if any, contact information is collected on church visitors now and what follow up efforts are made?"
- "Are there any other opportunities or events that might bring in new visitors?"

Working against you are a couple of key factors:

Except for the paid office staff, you will most likely be working with volunteers, so the pace of progress could be slow. Decisions "made by committee" usually are.

Second, they tend to be more price-conscience due to the nature of their "business." Still, churches represent a great sales opportunity and source of business revenue for you.

Within this vertical, you'll find everything from small-format color, to short-run digital, to direct mailings, to wide-format banners and posters. Don't be surprised if the church "Does their printing in-house." What they are typically referring to are the Sunday bulletins. You need to expand their definition of "printing."

Opportunity #4: Capital Campaigns

From time to time, churches hold a capital campaign. This might be a renovation (did you know that there are construction companies that specialize in painting and restoring church steeples?) or a new addition. It might even involve raising money for painting or repaving. Very often, churches engage fund-raising specialists to help them with their capital campaigns. These companies take a percentage of what's raised as compensation and guide the churches through the process. You won't find their name anywhere on the websites, but it is a good question to ask and something to be aware of.

Capital campaigns first require explanation and justification due to the large dollar amount. Digital/Inkjet color helps to tell the story either in the form of large format (if a live presentation is given) or small as part of a mailing announcing the initiative. Then there's VDP either as a simple mailing or something more complex that identifies potential donors.

Key Contact: is likely to be the Pastor or a Senior Warden/Church Elder.

Research: Most likely, this is spelled out on the website.

Opening Pitch: "The purpose of my call is to help the church with its capital campaign. We have resources available that go beyond standard print and mail. We can help sell the idea and then create a visual storyline."

The Questions to ask:
- "What is the goal of your capital campaign?"
- "Have you done anything like this recently?"
- "Are you handling this in-house or have you hired someone to run it?"
- "Who is in charge of this project?
- "Tell me about your database. Is it up-to-date and accurate?"

Like banks, many churches insist/prefer that you are a member of that faith—if not that church—in order to be a vendor. There are single churches, those loosely affiliated with a particular faith, and larger networks. The latter makes up the majority of this vertical: Catholic, Baptist, Lutheran, etc. The Catholic church often buys its Sunday worship materials from the local Diocese. Churches have some form of a member committee that runs things. It might be Vestry or Elders, for example. Invariably, one person on that committee has some level of marketing or advertising skills. Thus, they are instantly considered experts. Be aware of this fact and seek them out. There might be some strong ego issues to work around.

The key contact on staff is likely to be the Office Manager or Church Secretary. Larger projects might involve some of the church elders, such as Vestry or the Board (each denomination uses different language). To varying degrees, the Pastor is also an influencer, but do not automatically assume that he is running the show. They went to Divinity school, not business school. Generally speaking, Pastors are known to be either good orators or good administrators. Precious few are both.

One recommendation is that you log onto the church's website and hit the "Contact Us" button. Does it lead you directly to an email? How much personal information does it ask you? Does the church offer to send you any printed material? Is there a contact name shown? This information might come in handy when you finally do make contact. This step will also gain you insight into the church's commitment to growth and marketing plans.

One final entry point would come from special, one-off events such as conferences, trips or religious educational programs. Look under the "Calendar and Events" tab to see what you can find. Generally speaking, finding someone to talk to is fairly easy since their name should be listed somewhere on the description page.

You will likely find Churches to be particularly price-sensitive. This makes sense since they are trying to make the most of their financial resources and the fact that they are a non-profit. It's important that you have a conversation with your key contact so they understand that your ideas are meant to be yours and should not be bid out. If you're doing your job correctly, you'll come up with a good idea, and they will see the value in your work. They might force you to discount the price, but they will still reward you with the order as long as you are not too far off price-wise.

A second objection might have to do with the total spend. That is, if you present an idea for say, $10,000, they might not have the budget for that. Always have a lower-priced backup proposal, such as a $6,000 solution. By comparison, this will look to them like a bargain and you will find this second proposal to be less price-sensitive.

Opportunity #5: Special Events

One final opportunity to look for is special events for which large format banners and posters are required. If they are not listed on the website, you will learn about them by either visiting the church or asking the office. Make the staff aware of your capabilities.

Additional Resources

In August 2017, Idealliance hosted a valuable and well-attended webinar called, "What Churches Print and How You Can Benefit" and its actually pretty good. Members can view the recording through their website (but good luck finding it amongst the abyss).

Google "10 Marketing Mistakes that Churches Make" for some excellent background information.

VERTICAL MARKETS
#4 Education
Colleges, Universities, and Secondary Schools

Selling Digital/Inkjet to Education– Colleges, Universities, and Secondary Schools

Primary Business Needs

Modifying the three main revenue generators for this vertical, we come up with:

1. **Attracting more students**—Schools have an on-going need to find the next group of students. This might sound like a "so what?" point since all businesses face this same challenge but consider this: A four-year college loses 25% of its "customers" each year. Does that put the challenge into perspective?

2. **More revenue from existing students**—This is a much smaller opportunity since the business model isn't a menu of options; it's more like paying for a buffet.

3. **New markets**— Adding peripheral revenue generators:
   • Online education
   • Continuing education
   • Selling school pride through direct mail programs.

General Information and Digital/Inkjet Selling Opportunities:

The Education vertical provides a target-rich environment as schools still rely heavily on print—including digital/inkjet output—to meet their business needs. Bill might be biased, having gone through the college admissions process with each of his three girls, but he considers Education to be one of the most lucrative opportunities for a print sales rep (Kelly's kids are much younger. Someday, she'll see!). There is plenty of need and plenty of products and services to offer. From high school students requesting information, to Capital Campaigns, to keeping in contact with Alumni, print is very much alive in this sector.

Another interesting phenomenon that is unique to this vertical: Not all "customers" pay the same rate. A state school, for example, charges out of state students twice that of in-state, making the out of state prospects far more attractive financially. And schools also do a fair amount of international recruiting since those students typically pay full price with no scholarship dollars spent.

The biggest issue colleges/universities face at present has to do with cost, value, and ROI. Enrollment applications are down (2-3% annually according to the Wall Street Journal, Feb. 12, 2018), the cost of a four-year education is skyrocketing, and the average student loan amount for graduates in 2017 was a little under $39,400 (Source: U.S. Bureau of Statistics). To combat this, colleges and universities are getting more creative with their educational offerings and their financing options. Admissions directors face serious challenges in targeting the right students, focusing on those who show the most interest, and then doing everything they can to get the accepted students to commit. There is a sales opportunity for you along every step of the way.

Opportunity #1: Qualified High School Campaigns

High school students tend to request information on multiple colleges at once. For the student, this creates a blizzard of information during this very exciting time in their life. For the school, it's a bit of a nightmare since all of these "leads" are unqualified, leaving them to wonder which requests are from serious students and which are just kicking tires.

If student interest level could be tracked, those applicants who are more genuine can be better targeted. Similarly, by learning the interests of the particular student, specific marketing messages using variable data printing will highlight that aspect of the school. For example, a website that lists a series of potential interests—theater, hiking, debate, etc.—could then run into a mailing that emphasizes those school strengths.

Key Contacts: Admission Director

Research: Go to the website and request more information in the same way a high school junior or senior would. See what questions they ask about your interests, how long it takes for the request to be fulfilled, and what arrives in the mail. Keep track of all of this on a spreadsheet.

Your Opening Pitch: "The purpose of my call is to speak with you about identifying the most interested new potential students for your school. I can help you track interest, fulfill requests, and follow up with information relevant to the individual."

The Questions to Ask:

- "Who is your target student?"
- "What is your current approach to attracting new students?"
- "How effective has that been? Any measured results?"
- "Is attracting students a challenge for you?"
- "How important is financial aid in your Admissions process?"
- "After a student shows his or her interest in your school, how do you currently remain in touch?"
- "Tell me about your database. Is it up-to-date and accurate?"
- "Do you take a different approach regarding Continuing Education classes?

Stiff competition exists as schools fight for kids who have been accepted by multiple institutions and have numerous options. One Wall Street Journal article stated that a college /university will spend an average of $2,200 per accepted student in order to get that student to commit. Schools will hold events and bombard potential students with mailings (see the article link in the Additional Resources section), trying to convince them that they belong on their campus. Bill went to one such event in the spring of 2013 when his youngest daughter was accepted to the University of Connecticut. It was held in a large ballroom at a Marriott Hotel outside of Boston, and there were hundreds of students and parents in attendance. That couldn't have been cheap to host! Butler University even put their school mascot, a dog, on the road to inform select high school students they've been accepted. Admissions officers are traveling hundreds of miles to inform high school seniors they have been accepted to their college and to urge them to enroll. It's not just the star athletes or scholarship winners who get the personal treatment. It's pretty much anyone, a tactic driven by competition to snag the declining number of college-bound high school students.

Opportunity #2: Post-Acceptance Marketing

Digital/Inkjet printing's high quality in low quantities give schools the chance to send mailings designed to close the deal. College applicants who apply to a dozen schools might be accepted by half, giving them options but also forcing a choice. The competition for these students has been ramped up and digital/inkjet printing can help. Use the visual benefits of print to show accepted students what campus life looks like.

Key Contact: Admissions Director or any college representatives in the field (consult LinkedIn for names)

Research: Honestly, the best advice we can offer to learn more about this issue is to speak with an accepted student in your network and see what actions the schools take to close the deal.

Your Opening Pitch: "The purpose of my call is to help convince accepted students to commit to your school and reduce the amount of many your department spends on this important activity."

The Questions to Ask:
- "Once a student is accepted to your institution, what do you do in order to get them to actually commit?"
- "What is your school's success rate in this area?"

Small private and liberal arts schools, in particular, are struggling with enrollment (see "Cash Strapped Private Colleges Cut Programs, Sell Assets," *The Wall Street Journal*, September 1, 2017). Bill experienced this personally while attending a Parents' Orientation at his alma mater, UMass/Amherst, when his middle daughter Emma was starting. The speaker announced that the average GPA for incoming freshmen was a lofty 3.53. That was shocking! As Bill thought about this, he understood why: Simple economics. Mom and Dad can't afford to send their bright children to a private school at $45,000/yr., so they send them instead to a public school at less than half the price. This pushes out a lot of kids who ordinarily would have been accepted in to four-year public universities like UMass/Amherst and also causes great concern to private schools as those same kids then turn to smaller public, online, or two-year colleges.

Opportunity #3: Private Schools Enrollment

Public schools don't need your help (other than to attract higher-paying out of state and country students who pay higher tuition). Private schools do. Some are merging while other are closing their doors entirely. Scholarships are at an all-time high, dipping into endowment funds. Use digital/inkjet printing to help hone a message, learning first about the niche that private school serves.

Key Contacts: Admissions and the President

Research: It's hard to know from the outside which private schools are struggling with enrollment. Other than a Google search that might uncover a news article, there aren't a lot of public signs. The safe bet is to assume they are experiencing a drop-off in enrollment like everyone else.

The Questions to Ask:
- "Who is your target student?"
- "What is your current approach to attracting new students?"
- "How effective has that been? Any measured results?"
- "Is attracting students a challenge for you?"
- "How important is financial aid in your Admissions process?"
- "After a student shows his or her interest in your school, how do you currently remain in touch?"
- "Tell me about your database. Is it up-to-date and accurate?"

There is an interesting "game" that colleges and universities play regarding the U.S. News & World Report rankings that list the hardest schools to get into. Colleges figured out that by soliciting more students, getting them to apply, and then purposely rejecting them, their rankings would grow. This then makes a degree from the school look to be more valuable and, therefore, they can justify the high cost.

One of the hottest trends in the Admissions process is to request a two-minute video from the applicant.

Not sure if this is necessarily a trend, but an April 9, 2018, a *Wall Street Journal* article reported on a new trend of college alternatives, including the one-year college. One such school, MissionU in California, had 10,000 applications for 50 spots. At $14,000 and a 100% employment rate upon graduation, this is a story sure to have a future.

On the other end of acceptance is graduation and what comes next. It is the job of the Alumni Department to keep in touch with past graduates, primarily for fundraising purposes. The data is likely present, but Alumni Directors need help segmenting markets and sending more targeted messages, often incorporating variable data personalization, which makes it a perfect digital/inkjet application. They need help to stay in touch with alumni, as well.

Opportunity #4: Alumni Fundrasing Campaigns

Use digital/inkjet printing to create fundraising campaigns. Variable data printing, in particular, can help remind alumni about their glory days and favorite activities in the hopes they open their checkbooks.

Key Contact: Alumni Director

Research: All colleges and universities have Alumni interaction at some level, but some schools go so far as to get together in distant cities to watch football games and form LinkedIn groups. The school's website will give you some idea as to its Alumni involvement, group size, and strength. Look for upcoming activities/events and a contact name.

Your Opening Pitch: "The purpose of my call is to talk with you about how my company can help with Alumni engagement."

The Questions to Ask:
- "How do you currently track your alumni?"
- "How often do you mail to this group?"
- "How affective have your requests for donations been?
- "What is the accuracy of your database?"

One place to start is with your alma mater. They are certain to take your call and you can learn a great deal, cutting your teeth on this huge vertical market sales opportunity.

Opportunity #5: Tracking Interested Families

We include Private High Schools (a.k.a. Prep or Secondary Schools) because many of these same opportunities are transferable and applicable there. What's unique about this group, however, is that 80% of the kids that attend boarding schools live within 100 miles, and it's an even tighter range if it's day-only. These schools have clearly identified target markets and a long history of trying to attract the right kind of student, giving you a good opportunity to learn from what marketing outreach they've done already. There is a season to this vertical segment. Private high school fairs occur mostly in the fall.

Prep schools need help tracking interested parties. Families who visit a school are obviously interested enough to warrant the cost of using digital/inkjet printing for follow-up mailings.

Key contact: Admissions Director and field representatives

Research: The website will tell you when and where they are participating in informational fairs. Schools in the same area will rotate events each year, each taking a turn. You might consider attending to view their marketing material, learn more from the school's representatives, and put your name on some mailing lists.

Your Opening Pitch: "The purpose of my call is to help your school track interested families."

The Questions to Ask:

- "Who is your target student?"
- "What is your current approach to attracting new students?"
- "How effective has that been? Any measured results?"
- "Is attracting students a challenge for you?"
- "How important is financial aid in your Admissions process?"
- "After a student shows his or her interest in your school, how do you currently remain in touch?"
- "Tell me about your database. Is it up-to-date and accurate?"

Families who enroll one child into a school are far more likely to enroll additional children there, too. Use database management and digital/inkjet printing to stay in touch. This is a good point to bring up with Admissions Directors as a follow up opportunity.

We saw a great solution applied to the University of Wisconsin/Madison. Their School of Banking was trying to pitch a two-year postgraduate program. Using a combination of commercial and digital/VDP marketing, attendance increased 88%. A list of "Influencers" (alumni and local banking community CEOs) were sent a mailing with information on the program and informing them that anyone they thought might be interested should either call an 800 number or go online to visit a website. Just under 7,000 pieces were mailed out and they generated a little more than 1,000 names. Then, using a digital/inkjet press, customized postcards were sent out directing interested parties to a specific website. This was a very effective use of different print options and it yielded a successful and repeatable direct marketing solution.

Special events, such as Homecoming or the gathering of alumni in a faraway city to attend a football game, requires communication and organization. Look for local groups on LinkedIn. There will be the name of an event and the person who's organizing it.

Opportunity #6: Admissions Signage

Another opportunity in Admissions lies in signage. The Admissions office is typically well-furnished since potential students will make this their first stop.

Decorate the Admissions office with wallpaper wrap and interchangeable posters in the hallway to help the school make a great first impression on prospective students as they come for campus tours.

Key Contact: Admissions Director

Research: Get in the car. Drive to campus. Walk in to their Admissions Office and look around. How visually interesting is it?

Your Opening Pitch: "The purpose of my call is to speak with you about how my company can improve the look of your Admissions Office, creating a powerful visual image for prospective students and their family."

This sale is less of an inquiry that requires open-ended questions as it is a sit-down with the decision-maker to show samples of your work. You might consider bringing a camera on your campus visit, taking some pictures, and printing up a sample to use as part of your presentation.

Opportunity #7: Athletic departments

There are lots of opportunities here for signage. The key contact will be the Athletic Director.

Opportunity #8: Fill Empty Seats

Night school/continuing education and empty seats— We think this is a huge opportunity. Think about it: If a class has 50 chairs, but only 30 students attending, each empty seat represents 100% lost revenue. If the class costs $1,000, that $1,000 from the additional student goes right to the bottom line as there are no incremental costs associated with one more person in the classroom. So, if you can approach Admissions with the intent of helping them fill the room, you will find a ready ear.

Opportunity: Help the school to maximize their profit opportunities in continuing ed.

Key Contact: Admissions Director for Continuing Education

Research: Go online and check out their offerings. Request information and track the results.

Your Opening Pitch: "The purpose of my call is to speak with you about how my company fill up continuing ed. classes."

The Questions to Ask:
- "Who is the target market for your continuing education classes?"
- "How do people learn about them now?"
- "Do you track your marketing efforts?"
- "What is the status and accuracy of your data base?"

Additional Resources

There was an interesting article regarding how to communicate with prospective students in *The Huffington Post*. A key sound bite:

> "The Power of the Parents
> Regardless of the medium, the key to successful correspondence with prospective students is keeping parents informed, as well. Although an increasing amount of business is conducted online, John Chopka, vice president for enrollment management at Messiah College in Grantham, Pa., still believes that mailing hard copy information is the best way to get your message across."

Google "10 Marketing Mistakes that Colleges Make" for some excellent background information.

To stay current on this vertical, it is recommended that you read *The Wall Street Journal* on a regular basis; the newspaper covers the Higher Education market from the business side. You will need to read between the lines to find the opportunities. For example, one July 2017 article stated that financial aid given by private schools was at an all-time high in the 2016-2017 school year. This would suggest that smaller colleges may have priced themselves out of the market and might be struggling to find students. Another article from a few years ago indicated that applications in business schools were down 22%. That provides a perfect cue for you to call on Admissions to talk about ways to turn that around. Applying a little "Dale Carnegie thinking" (you can get what you want when you figure out what the other guy wants and help him to get it), the opportunity arises for those salespeople who can help schools solve these issues.

VERTICAL MARKETS
#5 Restaurants

Selling Digital/Inkjet to Restaurants

Primary Business Needs

1. More customers: Obtaining new patrons is the lifeblood of any organization and this vertical is no different. Restaurants use a variety of communication methods and mediums to build a brand and convince people to give them a try.
2. More from existing customers: Turning them into repeat diners. The only way a restaurant can survive is to create a following.
3. New markets: Adding peripheral revenue generators:
   - Catering
   - Take-out service
   - Meetings host
   - Food Truck

General Information and Digital/Inkjet Selling Opportunities:

Our suggestion for approaching a restaurant is to talk about the challenge of attracting new customers. If this is Number One on their mind, then it should be Number One on your mind, too.

Restaurants are a notoriously bad business model, with nearly 60% failing in the first year, according to researchers at Ohio State University, and 80% within five years. They suffer from stiff competition, as well as ineffective ownership with shallow pockets who don't realize the time it takes to build a base of customers.

In your area, you are likely to find a combination of chains, franchises, mom-and- pop establishments, standalones, and business entities/groups that own several restaurants. Since all types of restaurants have the same problems, all are good targets for you.

The primary business need and challenge of every restaurant is to get new diners through the door—get them to come once and then wow them with quality and service. That's the thinking anyway. The best way to do that? Retail research firm The NPD Group found that more than one third of dining decisions are based on deals and special offers.

Opportunity #1: Coupons and Direct Mail

For you, this means selling owners on the advantages of coupons and direct mail (especially EDDM or Every Door Direct Mail). By sending out a new offer that is valuable to them (a $25 gift certificate, 20% off the bill, buy one/get one free, free cocktail and appetizer with dinner, etc.), of low cost to the operator, and believable, recipients will walk through the door. If the restaurant can then impress them with good food and great service, loyalty should follow.

Key Contacts: Manager or Owner (if just one restaurant) or Marketing (if part of a restaurant group).

Research: It might be "Prospecting by driving around" or a Google search for new restaurants, but the idea is to identify them before they open their doors. The restaurant's website will then tell you when they are opening. For existing restaurants, locating prospects is much easier as this is one of Google's strengths.

Your Opening Pitch: "The purpose of my call is to help build traffic at your restaurant."

The Questions to Ask:

- "What is your current approach to getting people to try your restaurant for the first time?"
- "How effective has that been? Any measured results?"
- "How do new customers currently find you?"
- "Who is your target market?"
- "What do you consider to be the Number One reason why people try your restaurant for the first time?"
- "Tell me about your database. Is it up-to-date and accurate?"
- "Do you host or partner with any charity or community/civic events?"
- "Let's talk about the holidays. How are things different for you?"

Opportunity #2: Coupons ad Direct Mail

Another key factor to the success of a restaurant comes down to data. Even if it's just a fishbowl for business cards, restaurants need to collect information and then either create a dialogue with patrons (request feedback, testimonials, etc.) or promote repeat visits. Help with database collection, follow-up mailings, and special offers designed to get people to return.

Key Contacts: Manager or Owner (if just one restaurant) or Marketing (if part of a restaurant group).

Research: A restaurant's website will give you all the information needed here. Look for a mailing/emailing list to join. If they have one, join it. If not, there's your opportunity to help them start one.

Your Opening Pitch: "Repeat business is the lifeblood of any restaurant. The purpose of my call is to help you build a following by staying in touch with patrons."

The Questions to Ask:
- "What do you currently do to get people to return a second time?"
- "What do you do to collect personal data on your existing customers?"
- "What do you currently do to build a relationship, that is, start and maintain a dialogue with your customer base?"

Here's a personal example from a restaurant Bill used to go to in Marshfield, Massachusetts, years ago. When the bill came, it arrived with a card that promised a $5 coupon to help celebrate your birthday and anniversary. Just fill it out with contact information and they'd do the rest. Simple! It turned out to be a great promotion, especially with senior citizens. A smart one, too, because people would rarely come celebrate alone. That $5 coupon typically would be spread out over two to four people. Not a bad investment and it worked perfectly right up until the restaurant burned to the ground early one morning. Oh, well.

Not sure where or if this fits, but it came to mind so we'll throw it in: Years ago, Bill reprinted a blog (go to PIWorld.com and Search "How Real Business Owner Wants to Be Sold") that was written by a restaurant owner in Provo, Utah. He was talking about how bad salespeople are at following up. He'd started a new restaurant and had spent $15,000 on various sales schemes and gimmicks designed to help drive foot traffic. After each sale was made, the sales rep disappeared and never bothered to find out how the promotion went. The only marketing that worked, he said, was a printed flyer that he distributed himself (but even the sales rep who sold the flyers didn't follow up!).

Opportunity #3: "Food Porn"

No, we did not make that up. It's actually a thing! Print plays an integral role in showing potential customers what the dishes look like.

Everyone knows what a burger looks like, but a specialty restaurant that comes up with interesting recipes would benefit from photos of the food in either a mailing or posters. See and sell is a powerful marketing tool.

Key Contact: Restaurant Manager

Research: Check the restaurant's website to learn what kind of an emphasis they put on food quality and creativity.

Your Opening Pitch: "The purpose of my call is to speak with you about creating posters that feature your food options to help people understand what they are buying."

- "When a new dish is created, what does the restaurant do to promote it?"
- "Does your current menu have pictures? Have you noticed a correlation between the choices featured and the frequency they are ordered?"

Data collection—Own the data and you will own the customer. All restaurants will tell you that data collection is important, but few do it and even fewer do it right. If you can help collect data, you're in the best position possible to help a restaurant identify their key customers and to market special offers for special occasions (birthdays and anniversaries). We suggest you write an introductory letter discussing the value of data collection and presenting ideas on how it can be used. Then be sure to follow up.

Charities—Have you ever seen or heard of a restaurant that teams up with a local charity or civic group (a high school band or a youth group, for example) and donates 10-20% of the proceeds for a particular evening (typically a Monday, when business is slow anyway)? This presents a good win-win and is something that you can pitch and then support with printed matter to drive as many people as possible to the particular restaurant.

Co-sponsored promotions—Often times, vendors such as Budweiser or Tito's vodka will make money available to a restaurant to print up banners. You can find out by asking if there are any wide-format digital printing opportunities that the restaurant knows of.

Restaurant Groups— Example: www.patinagroup.com/private-events/corporate-events. These differ from chains in that they are a single company that owns several restaurants. Check out the web address example above and imagine yourself as a salesperson for that group. Your challenge would be to help fill those various venues with corporate events. A good solutions-based print salesperson could help!

Catering—Restaurants can expand their revenue opportunities through ventures like catering or even micro-locations like food trucks.

The typical objection you will hear comes down to two words: Prove it. That is, if you are pitching a marketing campaign, the restaurant will want to know how it can measure the success and ROI. Be prepared to provide that answer. Restaurant owners are not known for being good business people, so assume nothing and explain everything.

Additional Resources

Google "10 Marketing Mistakes that Restaurants Make" for some excellent background information.

Visit trade association websites to learn about the latest trends.

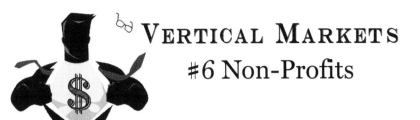

VERTICAL MARKETS
#6 Non-Profits

Note: The Non-profit vertical covers a lot of ground. They come in all different forms. Rather than choose one specific type, this research piece is focused on the fund-raising component of Non-profits.

Primary Business Needs

The three main revenue generators for this vertical are unlike traditional businesses in that they are seeking donation units (individuals or corporate organizations) instead of customers. They include:

1. New donors
2. More money from existing donors
3. New revenue opportunities—Non-profits are always on the lookout for a novel way to raise money.

General Information and Digital/Inkjet Selling Opportunities

Don't let the name fool you; there is money to be spent here! The term "non-profit" is a tax classification, not a goal. Companies that file as non-profit (there are 1.5 million of them!) have to meet certain guidelines and are regulated differently. They are unique in a lot of ways, but if they have the right types of projects, they can be quite lucrative for you.

The primary opportunity here is in fund-raising. While there are lots of organizations that consider themselves non-profits (a local town's youth softball league, for example), it's the more cause-based ones (Alzheimer's, cancer research, etc.) that are in most printers' crosshairs.

One key element to focus on when selling to this segment is "Value." Non-profits have limited budgets—more so than most other types of organizations—and can't just ramp-up sales or launch a new product when times get tough. Therefore, they need to make the most with what they have, so using words like "efficiency" in your sales pitch and proposals will speak to this fiscal restriction. Tip: Your ability to lighten their workload will go a long way to gaining business.

A good place to start is with a non-profit that is close to your own heart, especially if you have contributed time or money to that cause. Few people go to work for a non-profit for the compensation levels. They often do so because they have some kind of personal connection to its cause. If you have one as well, it will shine through and make a difference.

On that subject, volunteering is one of the best ways to gain access into a big fish account. From firsthand experience, we can tell you that slouches don't volunteer. That is, the kinds of people you want to talk to are also typically the kinds of people who donate their time to charitable organizations. Sales tip: Make note of the email addresses you see while in volunteer meetings. The person next to you might be the CEO of a huge company and you both are dedicated to the same cause. Instant rapport!

Another key element to the success of calling on non-profits is a printer's ability to handle data. Superior technical skills can supersede the need to be the lowest price. If you have any mad skills in this area, play that card!

Do your homework: Research the finances of the non-profit you are thinking about approaching. Also, research how to read their Form 990 financial statement. They might be a dot-org, but you aren't. As such, we assume you'd like to get paid for your efforts.

Network, network, network! Non-profits can be very well connected. You should be, too. Use your LinkedIn network to discover which companies might be connected with an organization you are trying to get into.

As for sales objections, the easy one here is, "Can you do any better on the price?" Note how that's different from, "Is that your best price?" or, "Your price is too high." You'd be hard-pressed to find a vertical market anywhere that is more price-sensitive than this one. Be prepared by addressing that objection up front, selling the value of what you're doing and pointing out the time-saving features as part of your proposal. It is also worth emphasizing ROI examples specific to the non-profit sector when dealing with the price objection issue. In the same way that you would for any direct mail piece, talk about the value of each response. "Sure, the campaign costs $5,000. But at a 3% response rate and an average gift of $100, that's a gain of $10,000. And a 3% response rate on a variable data campaign is extremely conservative.

Turn off the sales machine and be human. It was remarkable how many times this key takeaway surfaced in researching this vertical. Being authentic and showing genuine concern will go a long way. People who work at non-profits aren't in it for the money. They are in it with their hearts. Sales tip: Lead and sell with yours.

Of course, there is nothing like direct donations or donations in kind ($500 in printing, for example) to grease the skids. We suggest that you are strategic about it. Donate the signage for a golf tournament, but only if you can show up and make connections;

Corporate tie-ins—Companies are always looking for ways to get involved as a means to checking a box on their human resources checklist. Be aware of how and where this happens so that you gain possible access to that corporation.

The most effective nonprofits have a cycle:

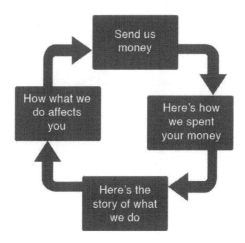

Opportunity: Sell to the cycle

Don't just sell a digital/inkjet order, sell a campaign. Each of the steps in this cycle represents a print application. Sales tip: While talking about one step, be thinking about the one before and the one after it.

Selling opportunities are specific to the activities currently undertaken by the non-profit (i.e., what they are presently doing to raise money), but here are a few of the more common endeavors:

Capital campaigns—These are big-ticket fundraisers that typically occur during a long period of time (12-18 months is not uncommon). Non-profits look for one-time donations and pledges that are paid over time.

Gala balls or dinners—These are fancy meals with high-ticket prices featuring silent/live auctions and lots of other ways to raise money. The need here is to spread the word and fill the chairs, including group sales to corporations that would potentially buy an entire table.

Events (Auction, Walkathon, Talent Show, Haunted House, Fashion Show, etc.)—Such one-off events might not seem like much, but they are excellent ways to collect data as different people will participate in different fundraisers.

Key Contacts: In each case, the Key Contacts are the Executive Director or Event Coordinator.

Research: Between the website and LinkedIn, you should be able to find the names of key contacts, the existence of any current campaigns, and dates for upcoming events.

Your Opening Pitch: "The purpose of my call is to speak with you about how my company can help you meet your fundraising goals both now and in the future. I'm less interested in selling you a print order as I am a campaign. With VDP, small and large format digital/inkjet capabilities, we have the firepower needed to be more than just a one-off vendor."

The Questions to Ask:
- "Who is your typical donor?"
- "What is your current approach to getting people to give money for the first time?"
- "How effective has that been? Any measured results?"

- "Why does someone typically support your non-profit?"
- "What are the different ways someone can support your non-profit?"
- "Tell me about your database. Is it up-to-date and accurate? How do you collect data and what information do you collect?"
- "Do you work/partner with any companies in the area?"
- "Are your fundraising efforts seasonal or cyclical in any way?"
- "Do you provide any kind of education regarding the nonprofit's goals?"
- "What percentage of people donate a second time?
- "What are you doing to encourage that? How effective has it been?"
- "How do you keep in touch with your donor base?"
- "What do you currently do to build a relationship, that is, start and maintain a dialogue with your donor base?"

Additional Resources

Google "10 Marketing Mistakes that Nonprofits Make" for some excellent background information.

This is where we leave you...

We are standing at a precipice and looking at a massive shift in the way we must look at our relationships with our clients and prospects. What used to work before won't work today. In fact, if it helps you, throw out the word sales and insert the word engagement wherever you see it today. The truth is that the more time goes by and the younger our customers get, the more evident it's going to be that the phone and our old methods just won't work.

We must stop asking the question "What's In it for me?" and start asking "how can I be of use?"

The focus of all our communications must be on educating, informing, and yes, even entertaining. Do that, and the sales will come. This is very counterintuitive to even what the two of us have been teaching you for the last two decades, but it's true.

People under 40 may not talk to you on the phone, but they will watch a video, or listen to a podcast, or look at your samples, or read your case study.

It's time to get into the content creation game, or at the very least it's time for you to become very good at curating content that is relevant to those you aim to serve.

A time for reinvention is upon you. Many of you do not like this. There have been so many changes in our industry in the past 20 years. And that change has been hard on us.

But we are still here. We are fighters. And the fighters and the winners win because they are willing to adapt and learn and change.

"If you don't like something, change it. If you can't change it, change your attitude." —Maya Angelou

We could throw a million great and relevant quotes at you about how change is good, but the truth is this: You wouldn't be reading this book if you were feeling 100% satisfied with how things are going for you and your company right now. You know your future is before you and that you have the power to change the course. So just by reading this book you are way ahead of the game.

Welcome to the change. Now get out there and make it happen.

Bill Farquharson & Kelly Mallozzi

Acknowledgements

The Authors would like to express special thanks to the following:

I would like to thank my co-author and industry bestie, Bill (a.k.a. the tall one), for being the best motivator, mentor and muse. Here's to another 15 years of friendship and partnership ou know, *all* the "-ships."— **Kelly Mallozzi**

To my co-author, Kelly, for agreeing to play literary volleyball with me, bouncing ideas, sections, files, and paragraphs back and forth until neither of us could remember which was the most recent version. I knew you had a unique understanding of this technology the first time we spoke some 15 years ago. Thank you for your input, contributions, and most of all, your friendship;

To my graphic designer, Allison Berry (BCreativeAF.com). You took 37,000 words and molded them into a book. You came up with a cover design that blew us all away. You brought your skills to the project and it's a better offering as a result. You truly are creative AF;

To Mark Michelson, Editor-in-Chief of Printing Impressions for your reality-check, "Hey Mark, does this sound right?" perspective when I called. Thank you for guiding us when we got too close to the content. You were the wise owl on a branch when we were looking at the trees, recommending that we step back and see the forest. Or something like that;

And finally, to Emily and Doug, who read the draft and added their two cents' worth. We'll sign and send two copies to you for free (the signatures double their value, you know)
— **Bill Farquharson**

Also from Bill Farquharson and AspireFor.com

The Sales Challenge —Where to look, What to say, How to create an effective prospecting process, Time mgt., Beating voicemail, Overcoming objections...and more. Increases, improves, and monitors your sales activity. $97/mo.

The 90 Day Sales Blitz — It's like hiring a Personal Trainer for your sales. Set and meet activity goals and improve your time management. $150/mo

One-on-One Coaching — For sales reps and owners. Great option for new reps. Call for pricing.

Live Presentations, Kick-off Meetings, and Workshops — Call or email for a list of presentation topics and pricing. Or, get on my calendar (see below) and let's talk.

More information is available at **AspireFor.com** To schedule an appointment with me, **go to www.meetme.so/BillFarquharson**

Also from Kelly Mallozzi and SuccessInPrint.net

Live Presentation Topics:
- Sell Like a Girl
- Gently Relentless - Persistent communication in a noisy world
- The Seven Habits of the Fantastically Terrible Boss

Services:
- Girls Who Print member mentoring
- Individual and Group Coaching
- More information is available at SuccessInPrint. net

Made in the USA
Middletown, DE
01 November 2018